Justin McCarthy

The History of Modern England

Before the Reform Bill

Justin McCarthy

The History of Modern England
Before the Reform Bill

ISBN/EAN: 9783741103551

Manufactured in Europe, USA, Canada, Australia, Japa

Cover: Foto ©ninafisch / pixelio.de

Manufactured and distributed by brebook publishing software (www.brebook.com)

Justin McCarthy

The History of Modern England

MODERN ENGLAND

BEFORE THE REFORM BILL

BY

JUSTIN McCARTHY, M.P.

AUTHOR OF "THE HISTORY OF OUR OWN TIMES," ETC.

London
T. FISHER UNWIN
PATERNOSTER SQUARE
NEW YORK: G. P. PUTNAM'S SONS
MDCCCXCIX

COPYRIGHT BY T. FISHER UNWIN, 1898
(For Great Britain).

COPYRIGHT BY G. P. PUTNAM'S SONS, 1898
(For the United States of America)

PREFACE

In this volume and in the one to follow my purpose is to give an account of the social and political development of England since the opening of the century. I do not attempt anything like a minute and detailed history of the events that followed each other during that time; and indeed my intention is rather to give something like a picture than to give to my readers a chronicle and a record. I have endeavoured to describe each remarkable political and social development, and to group the statesmen and philanthropists of every order by whom each development was assisted in its progress.

I have, while keeping in view the order of historical succession, endeavoured to make the story of each great reform, political or social, a story complete in itself, and disentangled as far as possible from the cluster and confusion of events that were passing all around it, and exterior to it. The true history of England during that long period of marvellous growth will be found to be the history of the country's progress in education, in science, and in the conditions that tend to make life useful, healthful, and happy. Successive changes in administration, the rivalries of statesmen at home and abroad, the barren wars which spring from the competing ambitions of dynasties are, after all, but the accidental difficulties in the way of man's improvement; and while they cannot be denied, their proportionate representation in history are sometimes dealt with as if they were the main events of history, and were entitled to occupy the largest space and foremost place in the picture drawn by the historian. My purpose has been something different from this; my desire has been to describe the marvellous changes wrought by science and literature, by statesmen and philanthropists in the social life of England during the wonderful century which is now drawing to a close. My wish has been to make my readers acquainted with the men who helped to bring about those changes, as well as with the nature, extent, and influence of the changes themselves; and thus to tell the story of England's nineteenth century in such a manner as to secure it an easy way to the understanding, and a place in the memory of even my youngest readers.

JUSTIN McCARTHY.

CONTENTS

I.

ARMS AND THE MAN . . . 1–9

Napoleon—"The Iron Duke."

II.

ENGLAND'S "BENEVOLENT DESPOT" . . . 10–35

The Younger Pitt—Charles James Fox—The Disappointments of Peace—Religious Disabilities—"The Democracy"—The King puts his foot down—The King's good points—Death of George III.

III.

IN THE WAKE OF THE PEACE . . . 36-65

The Congress of Vienna—Division of the spoil—The Holy Alliance—The Allied Sovereigns—George Canning—The Prince Regent—Needed Reforms—Lord Cochrane—Lord Eldon—Lord Castlereagh—Informers.

IV.

GEORGE IV. 66–87

What was thought of the King—Queen Caroline—The Duke of York—Peterloo—The Public Meeting—The Meeting broken up—"Some one had blundered"—Lord Eldon's Law—The right of Meeting.

V.

THE CATO STREET CONSPIRACY . . . 88–107

The Cato Street Conspiracy—Thistlewood—The Garret in Cato Street—The Battle of Bonnymuir—Execution of Thistlewood—"The world is not thy friend"—Anomalies of Representation—Old Sarum—Bribery and Corruption.

VI.

GEORGE CANNING 108–151

Canning's parents—Canning in Parliament—The *Anti-Jacobin*—Kotzebue's death—Canning's reply—The Congress of Verona—Canning's Plymouth speech—The Monroe Doctrine—Calling in the New World—Canning's Peace Policy—The Holy Alliance—Catholic Emancipation—The Greek struggle—"Go it, Ned!"—Canning and Huskisson—Canning's last illness—Huskisson's resignation—Huskisson's position.

VII.

RELIGIOUS DISABILITIES 152–190

The Dissenters—The Roman Catholics—Upon the True Faith of a Christian—The Catholic Association—Daniel O'Connell—The Clare Election—The Irish State Church—Sir Francis Burdett—Vesey Fitzgerald—"The serf of Clare"—Lord Anglesey's view—Lord Anglesey's dismissal—The Coronation Oath—The King's Question—"Checks and Balances."

VIII.

COMING REFORM CASTS ITS SHADOW BEFORE. 193–218

Charles the Tenth—The Dey of Algiers—Not revolt but revolution—William the Fourth—The Fall of Charles X.—The Princess Victoria—The Duke of Cumberland—Henry Brougham—The death of Huskisson—Alarmist predictions.

CONTENTS

IX.

THE GREAT REFORM BILL . . . 219–253

Popular excitement—Brougham and Russell—Grey and Brougham—Napoleon at Elba—The expected measure—Lord John Russell's speech — Rotten boroughs — The Government proposal—The New Franchise—Sir Robert Inglis — Sir Robert Peel — Peel against the Bill — Daniel O'Connell's speech—The policy of the Tories—The second reading—Parliament dissolves—The new Parliament.

X.

THE REFORM BILL AGAIN 254–284

Parliamentary obstruction—A Committee of obstruction—The House of Lords—Defeat in the Lords—Serious riots—If the King holds out — Execution of rioters — "The Waverers" — Lord Grey's resignation — The King's Unpopularity—The Royal Assent—Some great Conservatives—"Finality"—Farewell to Lord Grey.

XI.

SLAVERY—BLACK AND WHITE . . . 285–333

Anti-slavery leaders — "White slaves" — West Indian troubles—The Rev. John Smith—Anti-slavery resolutions—O'Connell's "No Compromise"—Domestic slavery—The arguments of the planters—Lord Ashley — Women and children in factories—Women in mines — Regulation of labour—Employer and workman—The "climbing boys"—"These almost clergy imps"—The master sweep—Impressment for the navy—The press-gang—Flogging in the navy—Time justifies abolition.

INDEX . 335

LIST OF ILLUSTRATIONS

GEORGE III.—*From a painting by Allan Ramsay, in the National Portrait Gallery* . . *Frontispiece*	
	PAGE
NAPOLEON	3
NELSON	7
WILLIAM PITT.—*From a painting by John Hoppner, R.A., in the National Portrait Gallery* . .	11
CHARLES JAMES FOX.—*From a painting by Karl Anton Hickel, in the National Portrait Gallery* .	15
RICHARD BRINSLEY SHERIDAN.—*From a painting by John Russell, R.A., in the National Portrait Gallery*	19
WILLIAM WORDSWORTH.—*From a portrait by Henry W. Pickersgill, R.A., in the National Portrait Gallery*	23
TRAFALGAR SQUARE	33
JOHN KEATS.—*From a painting by William Hilton, R.A., in the National Portrait Gallery* . .	43
LORD BROUGHAM.—*From a painting by James Lonsdale, in the National Portrait Gallery* .	53
LORD ELDON.—*From a painting by Sir Thomas Lawrence, P.R.A., in the National Portrait Gallery* .	57
SIR WALTER SCOTT.—*From a painting by Sir William Allan, R.A., in the National Portrait Gallery* .	61
GEORGE IV.—*From a painting by Sir Thomas Lawrence, P.R.A., in the National Portrait Gallery* .	67

	PAGE
QUEEN CAROLINE.—*From a painting by James Lonsdale, in the National Portrait Gallery*	71
ST. PAUL'S CATHEDRAL	99
RIGHT HON. GEORGE CANNING, M.P.—*From a bust by F. Chantrey, R.A., in the National Portrait Gallery*	109
GEORGE GROTE.—*From a painting by Thomas Stewardson, in the National Portrait Gallery*	115
LORD BYRON.—*From a painting by Richard Westall, R.A., in the National Portrait Gallery*	137
WELLINGTON	147
WESTMINSTER ABBEY	153
DANIEL O'CONNELL, M.P.—*From a painting by Bernard Mulrenin, R.H.A., in the National Portrait Gallery.*	165
RIGHT HON. SIR ROBERT PEEL, BART., M.P.—*From a painting by John Linnell, in the National Portrait Gallery*	177
JOSEPH MALLORD WILLIAM TURNER, R.A.	187
HOUSES OF PARLIAMENT	191
JOHN CONSTABLE, R.A.—*From a drawing by himself, in the National Portrait Gallery*	197
WINDSOR CASTLE	205
GENERAL SIR CHARLES JAMES NAPIER, G.C.B.—*From a sketch by George Jones, R.A., in the National Portrait Gallery.*	267
WILLIAM WILBERFORCE, M.P.—*From a picture by J. Rising*	291
LORD DERBY.—*From a drawing in chalk by Samuel Lawrence, in the National Portrait Gallery*	297
LORD MACAULAY.—*From a painting by Sir Francis Grant, P.R.A., in the National Portrait Gallery*	301
EARL OF SHAFTESBURY, K.G.—*From a bust, modelled by Sir John Edgar Boehm, Bart., R.A., in the National Portrait Gallery.*	309

I

ARMS AND THE MAN

IN the *Annual Register* for the year 1800 we find on the opening page of its preface a remarkable prophecy. "The Temple of Janus," says the preface, "is shut; it is not unreasonable to hope that it will be long before it be again opened. A dreadful but salutary experiment in the course of the last ten years has been made by the nations. The rulers of states and kingdoms have been taught the danger of tyranny; the people that of anarchy; the financier that even commercial advantages may be too dearly purchased; the politician and statesman that durable power consists not so much in extended territory as in compacted dominion, flourishing population, and above all in justice—justice in the conduct of governments external as well as internal. We are henceforth, we hope and doubt not, for many years, to be called from the horrors and miseries of war to progressive improvement in all the arts of peace; a nobler as well as a more pleasing and profitable career of ambition among civilised nations than that of conquest. The energy of our ingenious and lively neighbours will return to the arts and sciences with an elastic force proportioned to the misguided ardour that has too long propelled them to the ensanguined field of battle. Their improvements will be our gain, as ours also will be theirs."

This prophecy had not long been delivered before it became only too evident that it was to be miserably falsified by the events of the times. The settlement on which the *Annual Register* so confidently relied proved to be no settlement at all, and England and France were soon at war again. The fiercest days of all that long struggle were to come between 1800 and 1815. England had as her chief enemy then the greatest military figure that had appeared in the world's history since the days of Julius Cæsar. Napoleon Bonaparte hurried home from Egypt and obtained such powers as made him practically the dictator of France. We have had, of late years, a whole new literature devoted to the character and career of Napoleon Bonaparte. The secret cabinets of statesmen, the archives of ambassadorial offices, have poured out new masses of correspondence and manuscript of all kinds to throw fresh light on Napoleon's chapters of history. Yet, after all, the man remains much as he must have seemed in the eyes of impartial observers—if there were then any such observers—in his own days. We have long outgrown the age of the "Corsican ogre" theory. Caricature is itself caricatured by the grotesque and ridiculous illustration which found such favour with Englishmen in the days of George III.—the sketch which represented George as holding the Lilliputian Bonaparte on the palm of his hand, and trying to

NAPOLEON.

"size him up"—as the American phrase might put it—by the help of a field-glass. We know all that can be told us of Napoleon's defects, some monstrous, some ignoble, but we recognise the genius of the man, and we can hardly be surprised if there were English statesmen who firmly believed that there never could be peace in Europe while Napoleon was the ruler of France. Perhaps the illustration used at a much later period by Prevost-Paradol to describe the antagonism between France and Prussia thirty years ago might apply well enough to the antagonism between England under her government at the opening of the nineteenth century and France under the dictation of Napoleon Bonaparte. It was a case of the two express trains started from opposite extremes of the same line of railway; the collision and the crash must come. To do Napoleon justice it must be said that he did make overtures to England for the establishment of an honourable and a lasting peace. The English Government of the day did not believe that his word could be trusted, or his oath, and they rejected his approaches, or at least they stipulated for impossible preliminary conditions, such as a restoration of the Bourbons by the permission, and we may say the patronage, of Napoleon. The result was that the war broke out again with something like redoubled passion, and until the fall of Napoleon at Waterloo it knew no check or stay. It was altogether a question of opposing tendencies rather than opposing forces. Our Government were striving, unconsciously no doubt, to fight not merely against Napoleon, but against the whole impulses, principles, and tendencies of the French Revolution. Napoleon himself could no more have secured a throne in France to a Bourbon sovereign, to the principles of Bourbon sovereignty, than George III. could. It is idle now to speculate on what might have happened if George III. and his advisers had given full and fair consideration to the overtures of Napoleon. Undoubtedly they were wrong in not doing so, but being the men they were they could not have done so. The war had to go on. Happily for England she had at the head of her armies the one man in the world who was best qualified to stand out against Napoleon's passion of conquest. The Duke of Wellington had nothing like the creative or, we may call it if we like the aggressive, military genius of Napoleon. But he was the embodied genius of resistance. He had absolutely no military ambition whatever. His strong guiding force was simply a sense of duty to his King and to his country. In military as in civil affairs he was dominated by that same sense of duty. He had a patience which, as Macaulay says of a like quality in Warren Hastings, might sometimes be mistaken for the patience of stupidity; but those who counted on its being an evidence of stupidity were sure to be confounded in the end by the ever-watchful, sleepless intellect that was always on the alert to find a weak point in the plans, the policy, the strategy, and even the tactics of an opponent. The fates had brought the destructive and the conservative forces of command into direct antagonism in the persons of Napoleon and the Duke of Wellington. Wellington was nicknamed " the Iron

NELSON.

Duke," and the nickname was a terse and admirable description of his character. England's Continental allies, as we all know now, were at many momentous periods divided and distracted in council, and they had hardly amongst them any general who could really be said to belong to the first order of military command. England was no doubt divided somewhat in opinion as regards the prosecution of the war, and many of the noblest Englishmen were strongly of opinion that the overtures made by Napoleon for peace should be taken seriously and declared the subject of grave international consultation. But in what may be called the executive of the councils of England there was no division of opinion, and when "the Iron Duke" was told that the war must go on he asked no further questions, but entered the field and held his own position. So the war went on and on, until Wellington won the battle of Waterloo, and then all was over. Napoleon had suffered terrible losses and disasters by his ill-fated Russian campaign and by the defeat which the Continental allies were able to inflict upon him at Leipsic. Wellington's stroke at Waterloo was but as the "dagger of mercy" in the Middle Ages which brought about at one touch the doom that could not by any possibility be much longer averted. A great French writer declares that the main difference between Cæsar and Napoleon was, that Cæsar always knew what he could not do as well as what he could do, and that Napoleon believed himself capable of every triumph which he wished to accomplish. Napoleon had attempted the impossible, and he failed accordingly.

II

ENGLAND'S "BENEVOLENT DESPOT"

LET us see what was the condition of England at the time when Napoleon's career was drawing to its close. So long as the great war was going on England kept a united front to the enemy. But of course there were internal divisions of opinion. There was in domestic affairs what we should call a reform policy, and also an anti-reform or conservative policy. While the war was raging men's thoughts were turned away from anything like a systematic prosecution of the reform cause, and it would have been impossible to get the British Parliament to pay any serious attention to proposals for an improved financial system, for the equalisation of burdens on the different tax-paying classes, or for an improvement in the franchise and the general representative system. But there always were some men who did their very best to keep the reform light burning, even through the most agitating hours of continental war. The great leader of the Conservative party was William Pitt, son of the Earl of Chatham—public opinion is still divided as to which was the greater

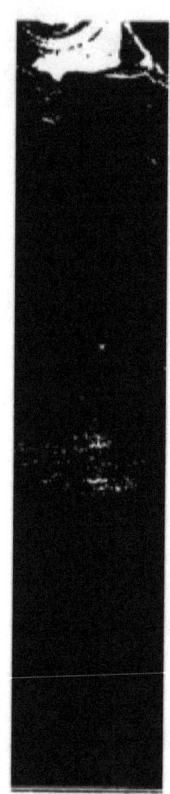

WILLIAM PITT.
(1759–1806.)

man, the elder Pitt or the younger. William Pitt the younger was undoubtedly one of the greatest statesmen and parliamentary orators England has ever known. He must be classed with Conservative statesmen, because some of the most momentous passages of his career were those in which he stood forth as the opponent of all projects of reform. Yet we know that Pitt was not by intellect or by nature an enemy of reform; he had himself foreshadowed and promised to favour some of the best reforms which it was left to other statesmen to accomplish—reforms which in his later days he had to oppose. Those later days were cast in the worst of all times for a reforming statesman. The thoughts of the country were absorbed in the war, and the war was sincerely regarded by many honest, stolid men, like George III. himself, as a calamity directly brought about by the crazy enthusiasm of French reformers. It was part of the creed of every country gentleman who followed Pitt in those days that if the King of France had only refused to listen to any wild talk about liberty and equality, about the abolition of class prerogatives, and the emancipation of public opinion—if he had only refused to listen to such ravings and ordered his cannoneers to do their duty, the Revolution would have been destroyed in its birth, and there would have been no occasion for a war with England. Therefore, these same country gentlemen who followed Pitt fully believed that every concession made to the demands of reformers in England would be nothing but an invitation for indulged reform to feast its thoughts on revolution.

All these seem to us very absurd ideas now, but we must remember that they were ideas which at one time got possession of and obscured the greatest political intellect of the day, the intellect of Edmund Burke. At all events, the King on the throne and the gentlemen in the provinces were of one mind on this subject, and they formed a power too strong for even Pitt to bear up against if he had been inclined to make the experiment. He was not during his later years inclined to make any such experiment. The war was too much for him; he died of it almost as literally as if he had fallen upon the field of battle. He never recovered from the shock which was given to him by the news of the great defeat of the allied powers by Bonaparte at Austerlitz. His friends said that from that time the "Austerlitz look" was always on his face.

Pitt's great opponent was Charles James Fox. It is a curious fact that in two succeeding generations there should have been in the English Parliament a Pitt fighting against a Fox. But though the second Pitt might well challenge comparison with the first, the second Fox was incomparably superior to his father, the elder Fox. Charles Fox was probably the greatest debater ever known to the House of Commons. He cannot be called the greatest orator while we remember Bolingbroke and the two Pitts and Sheridan, and in a later day Bright and Gladstone. But bearing all these illustrious names in mind the present writer still adheres to the opinion that Fox was the greatest of English debaters. His mind was informed by a generous enthusiasm for peace and for liberty.

CHARLES JAMES FOX.
(1749-1806.)

Thomas Moore, the Irish poet, well described him as an orator

> "On whose burning tongue
> Truth, peace, and freedom hung."

His bold, comprehensive mind surveyed the whole field of possible reform, and welcomed with eager sympathies every proposal which bore with it any practical promise of success. He was a reformer not merely for England, but for Ireland, for India, and for England's great colonial possessions. He, too, like his rival, William Pitt, was removed from the front of the political battle long before the fall of Napoleon gave the English people the chance of attending soberly to their own domestic affairs. One of the most brilliant speakers in the House of Commons was Richard Brinsley Sheridan— also the greatest dramatic author the English stage had known since the comedies of the Restoration. Sheridan's lustre as a parliamentary orator has somewhat dimmed, perhaps, of late years. No really authentic reports of his great speeches are preserved, and we find it hard to believe that even his famous "Begum" speech, the speech attacking the administration of Warren Hastings in India, can have deserved the strong praise which was undoubtedly given to it by all those who heard it, no matter what their political opinions—a praise which set it above any oration delivered in Parliament before. Sheridan clung to the reform cause even at the darkest hours of its history. Burke, who through the best years of his life had been a Whig, or what we should now call a Liberal, had quarrelled with Fox over the

French Revolution, and had declared in the House of Commons that the friendship between them was extinguished for ever. Sheridan remained fast to his old principles, but it was not given to him any more than it was to Fox to see a marked success accomplished in the difficult field of reform.

When the fall of Napoleon brought peace to Europe, that peace found England in a condition which might well have awakened despondency and almost despair in the minds of some of the best and wisest Englishmen. The country was almost starved; the want of work was felt everywhere, manufacturing industry had collapsed, and many of the provinces were traversed by gaunt and hungry patrols of workmen looking for employment, almost as distressing and alarming to meet as were the troops of the hungry whom Arthur Young might have seen during some seasons of the French Revolution. England was, for the time, practically exhausted by her war expenditure. The last three years of the struggle against Napoleon are estimated to have cost the English Treasury no less than £200,000,000 sterling. Then, to add to England's troubles, a tremendous disappointment had fallen upon the country with the close of the war. We all know by observation and experience what a semblance of immense prosperity is caused by a great war in all regions which it affects, except those alone which are made its immediate battle-field. The prosperity is purely artificial and fictitious; there is an immense and apparently inexhaustible demand for all the appliances and the provisions of war; an unnatural and ghastly show of trade and prosperity is conjured up,

RICHARD BRINSLEY SHERIDAN.
(1751–1816.)

and those who are not capable of looking even a little way before them are apt to think that the resources of the nation are positively inexhaustible. The State, however, meanwhile is not creating a vast prosperity, but only pledging its credit for an enormous debt. Thus it was with England when the wished-for peace had at last been brought about. The common belief, not unnaturally, was that with peace must come prosperity, and the disappointment was tremendous indeed when at first nothing but calamity seemed to be brought about. While the war was going on there was not merely the sham prosperity to keep up the spirits of the people, but there was the stress and ardour of the struggle to make all other considerations seem light when weighed in the balance with victory. The English people suddenly woke up from their fool's paradise to find that under certain conditions peace had her horrors scarcely less appalling than those of war. In truth, England found herself face to face with a crisis hardly less portentous than that which France had to encounter when she began her momentous work of revolution. Francis Horner, the great politician and economist of that day, wrote with some despondency about the wide and irreconcilable differences of opinion " between those who, on the one hand, will hear of nothing but to return to all that was undone by the French Revolution, and those who on the other hand, think that the French people have some right to make and to mend their Government for themselves." Francis Horner, be it remembered, was only speaking of those who may be called the moderate men on both sides ; he was not speaking of those, on the one hand, who would try to impose on the English people a system like that of the Bourbons in France, or, on the other hand, of those who were clamouring for liberty, equality, and fraternity, such as the French Democrats were striving to establish.

In truth, the story of England's nineteenth century is the story of the choice which at one time seemed to be imposed on England between revolution and reaction, and of the trials and troubles, the sad confusions, the many mistakes and blunders by the way, through which at last she was guided on the road to national prosperity. During the time of her struggle with Napoleon she had taken one decidedly backward step in the management of one department of her national affairs. Her ruling statesmen had succeeded in passing the Act of Union, which took from Ireland all control of her domestic affairs and compelled her to enter into an unwilling companionship with the Parliament at Westminster. England had also allowed herself to be drawn by a mistaken policy into a war with the young republic of the United States, out of which she only emerged by the tacit surrender of the one demand for the sake of which the war had been undertaken. She still adhered to the odious policy which denied the right of religious freedom to the Roman Catholics and the Dissenters of Great Britain and Ireland. Indeed, this latter policy was the immediate impulse to the Irish Rebellion of 1798 which was crushed after much bloodshed and was made the excuse for the passing of the Act of Union. We have said that "England" did all these things because there is no other convenient way of describing

WILLIAM WORDSWORTH.
(1770-1850.)

in ordinary language the influence which brought them about. But it is a most important part of our story that English people in general had no more to do with such principles or acts of policy than the peasantry of France had to do with the policy of Louis XIV. The vast majority of the English people, according to a favourite phrase of the time, had nothing to do with the laws but to obey them—or to disobey them, if they liked that better, at their own risk and peril. The Parliament at Westminster was in no conceivable sense the representative of the English people. It represented the territorial aristocracy and, to a certain extent, but only to a very limited extent, the wealthiest of the trading and manufacturing classes. No Roman Catholic, Dissenter, or Jew could be elected a member of that Parliament; when all other disqualifications were absent there was a property qualification which prevented any poor man from obtaining a seat in the House of Commons. It is curious to notice now that the reforming programme which was adopted by Charles Fox included amongst its leading principles, universal suffrage, abolition of the property qualification for members of the House of Commons, equal voting districts, and the introduction of vote by ballot at parliamentary elections. Fox, and those who thought with him, held that until these reforms had been carried Parliament could not possibly be regarded as the representative of the people's opinions and the guardian of the people's liberties. Half a century and more after the death of Fox these demands were still regarded by all steady-going Conservatives as the very extravagance of Radicalism, only fit for Chartists and Revolutionists and mob-orators and other such dangerous and monstrous creatures.

The very names of political parties have undergone a change since the days of Fox and Pitt. Fox was a Whig; Pitt in his least happy days was a Tory. The term Whig, when it is now applied at all, has quite a different significance from that which it bore when Fox was the Whig leader. Then it meant what we should now call an advanced Radical, a man in the front of every forward movement for popular rights and religious emancipation. Now, when it is used at all, it only means a lukewarm and backward Radical, who is scarcely to be distinguished from the more intelligent sort of Tory. Hardly any one now avows or admits himself to be a Tory, except as a sort of half-defiant joke. The Whigs of our time have become Liberals or Radicals; the Tories have settled down to be respectable Conservatives. We have, indeed, a great Democratic party growing up, which is perhaps destined to absorb both sections of Liberalism into its common denomination. In the preface to his interesting volume, "The Rise of Democracy," lately published, Mr. J. Holland Rose, the author, makes some observations with which this writer cordially agrees. "Throughout my inquiry," says Mr. Rose, "I have used the term Democracy in its strict sense as government by the people, and not in the slipshod way in which it is now too often employed to denote the wage-earning classes;" and he adds that "this misuse of the term is responsible for much slipshod thought on political matters." There has, indeed, been far too common a tendency of late years in England to use the phrase "the people" and "the democracy," as if the classes who work with their own hands at daily labour were alone spoken of when such words were used. The democracy to which the whole intelligence of England is now turning is that political condition in which the majority representing "the common sense of most," will finally decide the destinies of the State without the overruling dictation of any privileged class or order.

The close of the war found England governed by an oligarchy in the strictest sense of the word, and not by any means an enlightened or an unselfish oligarchy. The King, George III., was a man of very moderate abilities and an overweaning amount of obstinacy. Henry Erskine, the great Scottish advocate, political orator, and wit, said, many years ago, that what we call obstinacy in a donkey we call firmness in a king. We have grown, however, less courtly in our ways of late, and the tribute is so much the greater to the really good sovereign in whose praise we all unite. We may, therefore, speak frankly of the obstinacy of a king and say that this quality in George III. had nearly proved more than once the ruin of the country over which he had been appointed to rule. His was the influence which led to the quarrel with the American colonists and the war which ended in the independence of the United States. The King himself found the principle of policy, which, to adopt Johnson's mistaken words, declares "taxation" in that case "no tyranny," especially dear to his heart. His, too, was the influence which again and again prevented the concession of religious freedom to the Roman Catholics. This fact was made painfully evident on one memorable occasion. During the debates on the Act of Union with Ireland, Pitt made an attempt to conciliate some of the opponents of the measure by holding out more than once a hope that the union of the two Parliaments would be followed by some liberal concessions to the Catholic claims. Many of those who were strongly inclined to oppose the Government on this question withdrew their opposition in consequence of the promises held out by Pitt. But when the Act of Union was passed Pitt found it absolutely impossible to induce the King even to listen to his arguments in favour of the Catholic claims. The King went so far as to declare that any further importunity from Pitt on that subject would drive him back into one of his fits of madness. George insisted that he could not countenance the recognition of the Catholic claims without a violation of his Coronation Oath. It was humourously said at the time that England had now four instead of three estates in her constitutional realm— that whereas up to George's time she had only King, Lords, and Commons, she had now King, Lords, Commons, and Oath. George, in fact, threw his influence into every political question; he put into operation again and again the most momentous and seldom-used prerogatives of the Crown. He dissolved Parliaments and dismissed Ministers on the slightest provocation or pretext. If a majority of the House of Commons decided against the policy of his favourite Minister, the King took not the slightest notice of the decision, but maintained the Minister and the policy just as if nothing had happened. It would be hardly possible to conceive any course of royal action more entirely out of keeping with the constitutional usages of our day than such a stroke of policy as that often carried into effect by George III. The King, on one occasion when he was displeased with some public act or utterance on the part of Charles Fox, called for the Roll of the Privy Councillors, and with his own hand scratched out the name of the great Whig leader from the list.

England, in fact, had in George III. a sort of " benevolent despot," without the supreme attribute of royal intellect which is commonly understood to be a part of the ideal " benevolent despot's " outfit for the enterprise of government. It would have been well worth a revolution, could no other means have accomplished the object, for England to get rid of George III.'s cardinal principle of constitutional government. We shall see in the course of this volume how it fortunately came to pass that the English people were enabled to secure for themselves a constitutional and representative system of government without having recourse to revolution. Let it be remembered that the greatest intellects of the time were, with few exceptions, opposed to George III.'s ideas of principle and of policy. The course of action which led to the war with America was condemned to the end by the elder Pitt, the great Lord Chatham, and by Edmund Burke. The policy of conciliating the Roman Catholics was well known to be the policy of Pitt the younger, and it was only Pitt's unfortunate and almost servile submission to his master's dictatorship which enabled the King to hold his own for the time. If we ask ourselves why the conduct of King George did not bring about a revolution, we have to look for an answer to the conduct of his enemies as well as of his friends. In the first place, he was better served by all political parties at home than the unhappy Louis XVI. had ever been. Fox and Burke and Pitt, however they may have differed in other qualities, were all alike constitutional statesmen, and entirely opposed to any idea of domestic revolution. Then, again, the English people, as a whole, were much more patient in temper than the French, and indeed it must be owned that the English population of the poorer order had never had their patience tried so cruelly and so keenly as the patience of the French working classes had been. Moreover, we have just spoken of the conduct of the King's enemies, and it must be owned that nothing could have been more timely for the stability of George's throne than the wars with France, so long as they lasted. While Napoleon was still at the head of his armies, all thought of a revolution in England was out of the question. The heart and the nerves of the nation were braced up to the one great purpose of victory in that struggle, and the King was free for the time to play what antics he pleased with the constitution. We shall presently see that the more serious domestic difficulties came when the war was over and the return of peace gave sufferers time to ask themselves what they had got by it all, and to feel the full and lonely pressure of their grievances undiminished by the enthusiasm of a struggle with the foreign foe.

George III., it has been said, might have made, had he been more nobly endowed with intellect, a fair illustration of the ideal "benevolent despot." He was not in any sense of the word a bad man; he had none of the personal vices with which so many princes, here and everywhere else, have been spoiled. He was not a Louis XV. or a Charles II. He had a kindly heart, and, according to his lights, he endeavoured to do his duty as a husband and a father. He was a brave man—he had shown it over and over again—at least he had that kingly quality of courage which never fails when summoned on some great emergency. Over and over again his life had been attempted, for the most part, indeed, by maniacs, but he had never shown the slightest failure of nerve or of composure; and after all the knife or the bullet of a maniac may do work as deadly as the weapon of the sanest assassin. George never showed the slightest desire to deal harshly with those who made attempts on his life. He was himself the first on more than one occasion to suggest that the attempt was but the outcome of insanity, and his inclinations were always on the side of mercy. He showed many times that he could act with promptness and decision in cases of sudden and unforeseen difficulty. Nobody could have had less sympathy with the Catholic claims, and yet, when Lord George Gordon's "No Popery" riots broke out, and carried destruction to the homes of so many Catholics and their friends, the King insisted on the complete suppression of the outrages, and declared that if the riots were not put down within a certain time, he would himself take the command of the Life Guards, and charge the rioters in person. It has to be said, too, for George III., that he had not been well brought up in his home life, and some of his apologists are fond of arguing that even his very obstinacy was encouraged in him by his mother, who loved in his early days to impress on him that he must always show himself to be a king and make his word obeyed by his Ministers and by his people. He had long been liable to attacks in the head, and his reign was not very far advanced when the malady began to declare itself in the form of intermittent insanity. Soon after the outbreak of renewed hostilities with France one of these fits of madness came on, which led to long debates as to the necessity for appointing a Regent to take his place. The obvious and natural idea was, of course, that his son George, who afterwards succeeded him on the throne, should be put in his father's place while the father's malady lasted. But the hopes of many of the Whigs, of nearly all the friends of Catholic emancipation, and of most of the Irish people were already set upon George, the son, who had given promises of liberal inclinings which his after-life did not fulfil. A somewhat unseemly controversy was therefore raised in Parliament as to whether George, the son, was or was not entitled by constitutional right to assume his father's place during his father's incapacity for public business. Here, it must be owned, Fox and the Whigs made but a poor figure; they insisted on the absolute right

TRAFALGAR SQUARE.

of George, the son, while Pitt, on the other hand, upheld what might be thought to be naturally the Whig doctrine, and maintained that it was for the English Parliament to decide as to the proper person to act in the absence of the King. George, the son, was, of course, chosen for the place, and would have been so chosen in any case. The health of the King became worse and worse as years went on. He lost his sight; he lost his hearing; his madness increased, until at last he had to be kept under almost constant restraint, and was indeed much more thoroughly a madman than Shakespeare has pictured his King Lear. Poor George's death must have come as a relief to him in the end. Even the sternest historian may afford to be lenient with him. His end was less heroic, and even more tragic, than that of Louis XVI.

III

IN THE WAKE OF THE PEACE

IT is necessary to go back for a little in order to take a glance at the condition in which Europe was left by the Treaty of Vienna. That Treaty was agreed upon by the representatives of the European allies, and was already signed at the Congress of Vienna on the 9th of June, 1815. When the fall of Napoleon took place the Allied Powers had therefore little more to do than to proceed to put in action the general principles which were laid down by the Treaty of Vienna and by some previous agreements, and to settle the affairs of Europe according to their own convenience and good pleasure. There were other treaties and agreements also, which were found necessary to apply in various countries, in order to carry out the general arrangement. But we may, for the sake of clearness of expression, take it that the Treaty of Vienna made the grand settlement of European affairs after the fall of the French Empire. The Continent lay then before the plenipotentiaries of the great Powers like a corpse on the dissecting table, to adopt an expressive phrase, which was used much more lately, and with regard to a different subject. At first it was intended that France should be shut out from consultation or share in the new arrangement; but the ingenuity, the subtlety, the persuasiveness, and the perseverance of Talleyrand, the French statesman, succeeded in prevailing on the representatives of the great victorious Powers to allow France some voice in the settlement wherein her national interests were so profoundly concerned. The name of Talleyrand is one of the three great names which will always belong to the history of the French Revolution, the other two being those of Mirabeau and Napoleon. European statesmanship, up to that time, took no account of the feelings or wishes of nationalities and populations when coming to a settlement after a victorious war. When a party of gamesters have finished their night of play they simply count up the gains and losses and allocate the coins on the table. It naturally does not occur to them to consider whether the gold and silver pieces themselves have any feeling in the matter, and would prefer to remain with this player or to be handed over to that other. The statesmen assembled at the Congress of Vienna concerned themselves just as little about the sentiments and the predilections of the populations with whom they had to deal. Paris was at this time occupied by the soldiers of England and of Prussia. Louis XVIII., as it was agreed that he should be called, was put on his ancestral throne. The understanding was that the Bourbon monarchy was established for ever, and that there was an end for all time of any dream of Republic in France.

Napoleon surrendered himself to the captain of an English ship of war, and it is a curious fact well worth remembering that he was received with much cheering by a crowd of Englishmen on the quays of an English port, who had become aware of the great captive's identity. Napoleon was sent off to the Island of St. Helena, where he languished for a few years more, and meantime the work of European reconstruction went on. The Rhenish provinces were bestowed on Prussia, a rich gift, not, it must be owned, altogether unwisely bestowed. The Rhenish provinces were for the most part Catholic by religion, but the Prussian Government has never gone out of its way to intermeddle with the religious faith of its populations, and the provinces soon amalgamated thoroughly in national spirit with the general population of Prussia. The Prussian Government had even the good sense to leave the Code Napoleon where they found it in territories once occupied by France. Holland and Belgium were made into one Kingdom, the Kingdom of the Netherlands, under the rule of the House of Orange. This arrangement only held together for a very few years, and Holland and Belgium were enabled to effect a separation, mainly by the help of France, and each set up as a kingdom for itself. The difficulty which had stood so much in the way of the great Orange statesman, William the Silent—the difficulty of keeping Hollanders and Belgians together—was not likely to be got over by the decree of a number of statesmen recasting Europe at the Congress of Vienna. Prussia had been stripped of a vast portion of her territories by the Napoleonic conquests, and the statesmen of Vienna restored all the plunder to the Prussian dynasty. It did even more than that—it handed over to Prussia one-half of Saxony, and it gave her also a large portion of the old Duchy of Warsaw, the territory which we now call Prussian Poland. The greater part of Poland was handed over to Russia. Austria was endowed with the kingdom of Lombardy and Venice, and within less than half a century Austria, after tremendous losses in war, was compelled by the intervention of another Napoleon to disgorge part of her ill-gotten possessions, and thus allow Lombardy to open the way for a new kingdom of Italy. Genoa was annexed to Sardinia; the States of the Church were restored; and Naples and Sicily were handed back to the old Bourbon rulers. Russia and Austria came out of the transaction with the largest spoils, Prussia, for the most part, recovering only what she had held before the great war with France. England, to do her justice, sought for little or nothing, and obtained little or nothing by the arrangements of the Congress of Vienna. She had borne the heaviest and costliest part of the work; her navies on the ocean had defeated Napoleon at the very zenith of his power, and she had only her glory as a reward: let it be owned that the glory of English arms was never made more splendidly manifest than it was on the seas under Nelson and his comrades in battle. Few of the novelties set up by the Congress of Vienna held very long together. Austria had to go through a most troublous career—to surrender Lombardy to

French arms and Venetia to the arms of Prussia and of Sardinia. Prussia drove Austria, after seven weeks' war, out of the Germanic federation altogether. The elder branch of the Bourbons was ejected from the throne of France; the younger branch which succeeded only held that throne for eighteen years; then there was another French Republic, followed by another French Empire, which itself fell under the conquering hand of Prussia, and now once more a Republic prevails in France. The whole war against Napoleon was undertaken avowedly with the object of restoring the principle of legitimate monarchy to its old place in France, and rooting out for ever the growth of democracy and republicanism. Little more than half a century had passed before a Republic was again set up by the French people, and there does not now seem the slightest chance, come what else there may, of a Bourbon or an Orleans sovereign being thought of again by France.

The Holy Alliance, as it was afterwards called—the Alliance started by the Emperor of Russia, and joined in by the Emperor of Austria and the King of Prussia—proclaimed its mission. The Holy Alliance was a natural outcome of the principles and purposes which led up to the agreement made at the Congress of Vienna. It is well that the proclamations and the purposes of the Holy Alliance should not be allowed to fade from public memory. Sydney Smith forcibly and very justly spoke of the Sovereigns who made themselves into the Holy Alliance as "the crowned conspirators of Verona." The declaration of the Holy Alliance was contained in a manifesto issued by the Emperor of Russia from St. Petersburg and bearing date on the day of the birth of our Saviour, the 25th of December, 1815. In this proclamation the Emperor ordered that the Convention concluded at Paris on the 26th of September, 1815, should be read in all the churches throughout his dominions. This was the Convention of the Holy Alliance. It was arranged between the Emperor of Russia, the Emperor of Austria, and the King of Prussia. These Sovereigns, to quote from the words of the Convention, " solemnly declare that the present act has no other object than to publish in the face of the whole world their fixed resolution, both in the administration of their respective States and in their political relations with every other Government, to take for their sole guide the precepts of the Holy Religion of our Saviour— namely, the precepts of justice, Christian charity, and peace, which, far from being applicable only to private concerns, must have an immediate influence on the Councils of Princes and guide all their steps, as being the only means of consolidating human institutions and remedying their imperfections." The Sovereigns therefore pledged themselves to "remain united by the bonds of a true and indissoluble fraternity, and to use their arms to protect religion, peace, and justice." Then the Convention went on to explain that it was not by any means the intention of the Sovereigns who signed it to limit the blessings of those counsels of perfection to the uses of the Holy Allies only, and to leave all other European States out in the cold. On the contrary, the document contained the cheering intelligence that "all

Powers which were willing solemnly to avow the sacred principles which have dictated the present act will be received with equal ardour and affection into this Holy Alliance."

The world was not long left in suspense as to the inner meaning of this agreement. The Emperor of Russia, the Emperor of Austria, and the King of Prussia had their own ideas as to the way in which peace, religion, and justice were to be maintained. Peace was, in the opinion of these Allied Powers, to be secured by enslaving their own peoples and every population which was to be put under their control. Religion meant the Divine right of Sovereigns to govern according to their own despotic humours. Justice consisted in the suppression of free speech and of every other popular right or demand, in order that subjects might be taught to know their place, and compelled to keep in the position to which it had pleased the Congress of Vienna to call them. In other words, as a modern writer has described the situation, the crowned conspirators " proclaimed themselves the champions and ministers of religion and justice, but reserved to themselves the right of defining what religion and justice were." " Show me the man, and I'll show you the law," was a bitter old Scottish saying. "Show me the Sovereigns, and I'll show you the religion, law, and justice," would have been a saying strictly applicable to the Holy Alliance. The Sovereigns bound themselves to unite in putting down revolutionary agitation wherever it might upheave itself, and we all know what they would have defined as revolutionary agitation. Every State

JOHN KEATS.
(1795–1821.)

which should afterwards join the Alliance would be understood to have pledged itself to lend the aid of its arms and its troops to put down whatever might be defined as revolutionary agitation. The deliberate purpose of the Holy Alliance was to restore the dethroned Princes and Grand Dukes everywhere, to set up again the Divine right of Kings in France and everywhere else over which their power extended, to bring back to France the old days and the old ways of the Bourbon, and to establish as the reign of law the principle that one despot was bound to assist another in maintaining a despotic authority ; but that one people was not free to help itself or any other people to liberty.

The Holy Alliance, in fact, quite overdid its work. The Allied Sovereigns took no account of time ; the season was not one when an enlightened philosophy had much influence over political action ; and the two Emperors and the King did not understand that there was anything like a law of political development. So they went to work with their cheery faith in their own power to stop the movement of time and the process of growth. The influence they afterwards obtained over the Councils of reactionary dynasties in France and Spain became the principal means of upsetting the whole fabric on which the Holy Alliance was founded. When the Duke of Wellington heard of the Treaty, he gave it but a cold reception, and said something to the effect that he thought the Sovereign and the Government of England would ask for a somewhat more explicit and practical statement as to the actual purposes of the Alliance.

There can, however, be little doubt that the feelings of those most immediately around the English Sovereign would have led them far on the way with the work of the Holy Alliance. In point of fact, for a time such Ministers as Lord Liverpool and Lord Castlereagh were very willing indeed that England should lend herself to the conspiracy of Verona. It was only when Canning came into power that a complete severance took place, once for all, between the policy of England in foreign affairs and the principles of the Holy Alliance. Even if England had joined in the conspiracy, it is utterly impossible that it could have held its own for any considerable length of time. The genuine principle of democracy was, indeed, a little out of favour, even in England, at the date when the two Emperors and the King signed their portentous Treaty. The excesses of the French Revolution and the military dictatorship of Napoleon had aroused an immense alarm all through England and everywhere else. It cannot be questioned that even in domestic policy the mind of Pitt was greatly affected by the influence of this alarm. Reforms were delayed in England because of the difficulty which the mind of the average man had in distinguishing between a demand for a reform and a clamour for a revolution. But the democratic reform must have begun to develop before long, if all the Sovereigns of Europe had been combined against it. Democratic reform, to apply to it the noble language of Wordsworth's sonnet, had "great allies," its "friends were exultations, agonies, and love, and man's unconquerable mind."

We shall show before long how it was reserved for the best days of Canning's foreign policy not merely to withdraw England from any confederacy with the Holy Alliance, but to checkmate altogether some of its most important and most audacious enterprises. With Canning, it may fairly be said, is to begin the modern era of English foreign policy. It would be idle now to enter into any speculation as to what might have happened if the English statesmanship of that day had been more like the English statesmanship of a later day. It is still a question of keen argument whether the war between France and England was really forced on by England or by France. Some enlightened English writers, who cannot be suspected of any lack of patriotic feeling, insist that but for the policy and obstinacy of George III. there never might have been a war with France. English statesmen have learned much since then. The hero of the Iliad proclaims, at least in Pope's version, that " no more Achilles draws his conquering sword in any woman's cause." English statesmanship, we may well believe, will never again draw its sword in the cause of any foreign dynasty. So far as that goes, at least, the principle of non-intervention may safely be said to be established as a canon of British policy.

The settlement of international peace was followed in England by something very like an outbreak of domestic war. When great suffering prevails among a population, the first thought of the sufferers is, naturally, to look to the Government for an immediate redress of the evil. Disraeli once said that no

English Government, however popular, could stand up against a third bad harvest. The saying, of course, like most of Disraeli's sayings, was meant to be a sort of cynical epigram; but there was meaning in it for all that. Popular suffering will always mean political discontent, and political discontent, here, there, and everywhere, is discontent with the existing Government. The great Italian statesman, Count Cavour, used to maintain that national prosperity or national adversity was only a question of good or bad government. Perhaps this was giving somewhat too wide an application to a principle sound and healthy within its limits; but it certainly is a principle which cannot be borne too constantly in the minds of the rulers of men. After the close of the great war the English populations found themselves oppressed by poverty, by want of employment, and in many regions by absolute starvation. Employment had, to a great extent, collapsed; the price of food was enormously high, and was kept high, with the avowed purpose of enabling the landlords to maintain their rents. Bad weather added to the troubles; masses of agricultural labourers and of artisans in cities were clamouring for a reduction in the prices of grain and meat. These assemblages led to disturbances, and to night attacks on the houses of landlords and magistrates. In many places the wealthier inhabitants were compelled to abandon their houses for a time, in order to save their families and themselves from violence at the hand of hunger-maddened mobs. Many of the rioters were captured and put to trial, and, according to the ferocious criminal code of the time, several were sentenced to death, and actually executed. Rioting took another form as well. The rapid introduction of machinery into so many manufactories seemed to illiterate artisans but another means of lowering the wages of the working man. Here and there manufactories were attacked and machinery was destroyed, and the law did all that it could, in the way of severity of punishment; but severity of punishment does not feed half-starving men, or convince the intelligence of those who, while taking no actual part in riot, are yet in sympathy with others who, driven by hunger, seek any means, however desperate, of bringing about a better condition of things. Under the conditions that prevailed, tumult and riot were humanly inevitable, and at that time the ruling authorities had no idea of dealing with discontent except by the prison cell, the transport ship, and the gallows. Then, again, there was much rancour and bitterness occasioned at one time by the reports, only too well founded, which went abroad over the country, concerning the extravagance of the Prince Regent and his Court. George, the Regent, was living in a style which might have served the tastes of an Eastern despot or a Prince of the Lower Empire. The stories told about his luxury, his reckless and wanton extravagance, his monstrous debts, were only too well borne out by the nature of the incessant applications made to the House of Commons for new grants to save him from bankruptcy. It may easily be understood how the bitterness of want amongst the working populations was made more and more intense by the increasing knowledge of the Regent's outrageous expenditure. Byron wrote in sarcastic anger of the one comfort still left to a patriot nation, the consoling thought that—

> "Gaunt famine never can approach the throne,
>   Though Ireland starve, great George weighs twenty stone."

For some time the expression of national discontent did not shape itself into the lineaments of a deliberate demand for political reform. Food, work, and wages were the first concessions for which the popular voice cried out. It was in the beginning but a wild cry of agony; it soon awakened echoes from the voices of men who knew how to give its plaint a distinct tone and definite purpose. Probably the first successful attempt to put the popular complaint into a definite political form came from the teachings of William Cobbett. Cobbett was emphatically a man of the people: he was born among the people; he had been for several years a soldier in the army, and had served in Canada. He had been a bookseller in New York and Philadelphia. He was master of a style singularly telling. His language was as clear, straightforward Anglo-Saxon as that of Swift himself. His ideas were sometimes wild; he was not what would be called an educated man; he knew little of constitutional systems, and political economy had not become a popular science in his time. But he knew enough to know that many of the evils of which Englishmen then complained were to be ascribed directly and almost altogether to a bad system of government. His mode of reform was simple and drastic. He would have had one single legislative chamber elected by ballot and by universal suffrage. He became what we should now call an agitator. He threw his soul into the movement for political reform. He started a newspaper, which at one time was circulated all over the country, and was read in every garret and every cottage—those who could read declaiming his sentences to those who could not. He soon became a power in the land, and, to do him justice, he did not use his power unscrupulously or even, as far as his lights went, unwisely.

The great reforms which England then needed were: the reform of the constitutional system, the reform of the criminal code, the abolition of abuses in the Court of Chancery, the reform of the financial system, the reconstruction of the poor laws, and the removal of all the obstacles which interfered with the spread of popular education and the free expression of political opinion. There were many great reformers, both inside and outside the House of Commons, who had long been labouring hard in the best way they could for the remedy of the national grievances. At the head of the political reformers of this class the name of Lord Brougham must be undoubtedly placed. The fame of Lord Brougham has somewhat faded of late years. Perhaps Brougham lived rather too long for his fame. Those of us who can still remember him have a memory rather of the eccentricities and extravagances of his later years which sometimes put away from recollection the thought of those brighter and more distant days when Brougham stood forth as the foremost, the fearless, the indomitable, and the incorruptible champion of every great measure of reform which the needs of the country demanded. Brougham was undoubtedly a man of genius—no other word could properly describe him. Despite an almost repulsive appearance, despite his ungainly and fantastic gestures and his exuberance of language and of utterance, he was undoubtedly a great orator. A vehement, passionate nature carried him away in debate, sometimes beyond the ordinary rules of decorum and even of decency. This kind of passion grew and grew upon him, until at a later period of his career his friends began to dread that it might develop into an actual mental malady. But, whatever his defects, it is certain that he was not surpassed, and hardly equalled, by any man in his best days for the services which he rendered to the cause of reform. He was thoroughgoing in his denunciation of the slavery system, of the existing criminal code, of the financial abuses, and of the evils in the Court of Chancery. Another great reformer, especially as regarded the slave system and the criminal code, was Sir Samuel Romilly, whose family name has since become the synonym for the purest order of philanthropical reformer. Some of the men whose names we chiefly associate of later years with the cause of political reform, such men as Charles Earl Grey and Lord John Russell, had not come yet quite to the front. Sir Francis Burdett, a man of property and station, was for a time a great political reformer, and was for a time idolised by all popular reformers

LORD BROUGHAM.
(1779–1868)

outside Parliament. Nor must we omit from a list of those who then championed political reforms the name of the gallant Lord Cochrane, afterwards the Earl of Dundonald, the last of England's great sea-kings, before the days of steam and iron armour and heavy metalled guns. No man ever served his country more faithfully than Cochrane, and his reward was a charge of fraudulent conspiracy, an unsatisfactory trial, and a cruel degradation. He had given as much trouble to the French during the great war as any naval commander short of Nelson himself. He sat in the House of Commons as member for Westminster in companionship with Sir Francis Burdett, and a more staunch and resolute popular reformer never lived. It is well to know that the injustice of Cochrane's conviction was recognised in the reign of William IV., by whom he was restored to his rank in the navy. It remained for the present Sovereign to give him back all the honours and dignities which he had earned so well, and of which he had been so undeservedly deprived, partly, as the popular belief went, through the hatred of the Regent and his Court. Among the conspicuous reformers of those early days may be mentioned one who at the time acquired a sort of fame as "Orator Hunt." Hunt was a demagogue in the genuine sense of the word, and had the advantage, almost indispensable to a demagogue, of a thrilling and tremendous voice. Hunt organised and presided over all manner of meetings, out of doors and indoors, to champion the popular doctrines of democracy. He was elected to the House of

Commons later on, and sat there for some years ; but he did not maintain there his reputation as an orator. He did not, to use a familiar phrase, " go down " with the House of Commons. That House has a merciless way of pricking a bubble reputation ; and it has had, for many generations, at all events, the credit of being impartial in its estimate of the merits of a speech. Hunt was a failure in the House ; but he made a certain mark on the political history of his day, and his name is even still remembered by those who are fond of tracking out the progress of the reform movement in England. Another man—a very different kind of man—whose name well deserves to be remembered among the best philanthropists and reformers of that time, was Samuel Whitbread. Whitbread was a man thoroughly unselfish, a man of the highest character and the noblest aims. His descendant, another Samuel Whitbread, well worthy of the name, has but lately retired from parliamentary life, and will always be remembered in the history of the House of Commons.

These were the more prominent among the advanced Liberals of the time. Let us now see who were the leading opponents of reform. First of all came George III., who, while he had senses enough left to take any part in the rule of the State, was an unteachable and indomitable opponent of every movement which made for political progress. Next, perhaps, in constitutional dignity came John Scott, Lord Eldon, for many years Lord Chancellor of England. Lord Eldon was a man of very high ability, a lawyer of unsurpassed keenness and pro-

LORD ELDON.
(1751–1838.)

fundity, a man of unselfish character, where prejudice and passion did not obtain the mastery over his reason and over his moral nature. It is much to be doubted whether the whole English-speaking race could just now produce alive such a specimen of Toryism as Lord Eldon was then. The one main purpose of Eldon's life seemed to be to keep the political constitution of England exactly as it was without the slightest change. He was actually steeped and soaked in the belief about the wisdom of our ancestors. To Lord Eldon's mind, it would seem that our ancestors were a race of divinely inspired beings who, like the sovereign, could do no wrong, and whose laws it was out of the power of mortal man to improve. It probably did not occur to him to think that a day might dawn when, supposing the reformers to work their will with the constitution, the policy of those dreaded reformers might come to be regarded as the wisdom of our ancestors by some future Lord Eldon. No doubt, if any such idea had ever intruded upon his mind, he would have driven it away as a sacrilegious and a Satanically inspired thought. No man, it was humorously said, ever could be so wise as Lord Thurlow, a former Tory Chancellor, looked. Certainly no man could ever be so wise and so virtuous as Lord Eldon believed himself to be. So Lord Eldon went on opposing all reform, maintaining and championing every abuse in the electoral system and in the Court of Chancery, putting every obstacle he could in the path of any and every movement which tended to equalise the political position of class and class, and treating even the most moderate efforts of Liberal reformers as if they were the work of recognised enemies of the human race. It was well said by a brilliant writer that it had never been the fortune of any man to have an opportunity of doing so much good as Eldon had prevented. The Prime Minister during a great part of Eldon's time was Lord Liverpool, a man whose name will always be remembered as that of one of the most bitter opponents of constitutional reform, even in those bitter anti-reforming days. Liverpool seemed to know of only one way by which a popular demand for reform could be dealt with, and that was by the passing of new Acts for the most stringent repression of all popular demonstration. He was the author of a famous series of measures known technically as the "Six Acts," and by that title well remembered among English readers of the present day, the six Acts being a series of six legislative enactments brought in with the special and avowed purpose of making any manner of popular demonstration liable to be punished as an offence against the Crown, the constitution, and society in general. Studying his history and his character as well as one can at this distance of time, it seems hard indeed to understand what claim Lord Liverpool had to be considered a statesman at all. Some of his colleagues were worthy of such companionship. Lord Sidmouth, the Home Secretary, had once been well known as Mr. Addington, and in that capacity, through the influence of Pitt, had been raised to the dignity of Speaker of the House of Commons. Some humorous person of the time

SIR WALTER SCOTT.
(1771-1832.)

disposed of the relative positions of Pitt and Addington by a couple of lines very popular in their day, which proclaimed that " Pitt is to Addington, what London is to Paddington "—Paddington being then a very small suburb indeed. No doubt the temptation of the obvious rhyme had much to do with the inspiration of the verse ; but in any case the comparison was well balanced and effective. Neither Lord Liverpool nor Lord Sidmouth had ever given any evidence, we will not say of statesmanship, but even of parliamentary aptitude. Associated with them was Lord Castlereagh, afterwards Marquis of Londonderry, a man of much greater ability than Sidmouth or Liverpool, but of yet sterner order of mind, a darker and a fiercer spirit, whose name is not likely to be soon forgotten in English political history. We have to turn to the writings of the time in order to understand what was the hatred with which Lord Castlereagh was regarded by most of the leading Liberals of his day. Byron described him as a " wretch never named but with curses and jeers." Byron, it is to be regretted, assailed him in words even more brutal than these—words which will not now bear quotation. Even Lord Castlereagh's sudden death by his own hand, in a moment of temporary unsettlement, did not silence altogether the voices of hatred. The story of England's nineteenth century brings with it, at all events, the cheering fact that we have learnt to deal with our political enemies in a more tolerant and a more Christian-like spirit than that which found only too much favour on both sides of politics for many years after the time at which this volume begins. No speaker on a platform, no writer in a newspaper, would be tolerated now who allowed himself to indulge even once in the passion of personal invective against a political opponent, which was common, even among men of education and position, during the earlier years of the present century.

Here, then, we have the rival forces arrayed—the Liberals and the Conservatives, if we may transfer to the warfare of our ancestors the phraseology of the present day. For years we read of little or nothing but the holding of great public meetings to advocate the cause of reform, and the breaking up of these meetings, and the prosecution and the imprisonment of those who took a leading part in them. The Government of the day believed, or affected to believe, that the meetings were organised with the definite purpose of promoting a regular revolutionary movement all over the country. There can be no doubt that in some instances there was much violence of language, and even some violence of action, on the part of the agitators. In many places a certain system of rough drilling was unquestionably going on; but it was pleaded on the part of the reformers that the drilling was nothing more than a natural and convenient way of teaching untaught and awkward men, village rustics or town artisans, how to keep step in a procession, and how to shift their quarters according to the orders of their leaders from a position which was found unsuitable to one which was better suited for the orators and the listeners alike. Charges of the darkest kind were undoubtedly made, and with much show of reason, against the Government and its officials. It was alleged that not only were the authorities in London willing to accept the evidence of the basest wretches who offered themselves as informers to disclose revolutionary plots, but that emissaries of the Government itself had in many cases hired and paid such creatures to go about among the reformers and try to get up insurrectionary plots in order that they might betray them to the officers of the law. There certainly did seem to be in many cases only too much reason to believe that some such base system was one of the weapons of the home Government.

IV

GEORGE IV

GEORGE III. died in 1820, and as a matter of course George IV. succeeded to the throne. The new King had ruled so long during the eclipse of his father that his formal elevation to the sovereign power did not make much change in the actual conditions. George IV. had been brought up by his father on narrow, old-fashioned, stinted principles of education. He had a greater amount of natural ability than was given to George III.; but he had not the elder King's purity of personal character. Something might have been made of George IV. under a better and more liberal sort of training in his early days; but the effort to oppress him or to coerce him into a pattern son proved, as under such conditions it must have proved, a decided failure. His instincts and inclinations were generous; and he was at least capable of understanding a better political system than that which seemed perfection to the dull eyes of George III. There must have been much charm of manner and some brilliancy in conversation and style of George IV., seeing that he

GEORGE IV.
(1762–1830.)

became in his early days the close companion of men like Fox and Sheridan. It is out of all reason to suppose that such men as Fox and Sheridan could have clung to the companionship of a mere worthless profligate simply because he happened to be a Prince Regent or a King.

It is certain that at one time these men and others had great hopes that the accession of George IV. would prove a blessing to the cause of progress and to the nation. The eyes of the Catholics turned to George IV. as to a man all but pledged to favour a settlement of their claims. The Irish people in general believed that he was likely to encourage some better system of government for Ireland than the mere rule of coercion laws and the stifling of every popular utterance. There were, indeed, some Englishmen of advanced opinions who never trusted him from the first; but on the whole it may be taken for granted that there was among the public in general every disposition to give him a fair chance, and to accept his coming as the hopeful indication of a better time. Of course the private life of George when Regent had been one of utter prodigality and reckless dissipation. We must not attempt to try the private life of a sovereign in those days by the standard which happily prevails in our own. It was not at that time accounted a disgrace, even to a great statesman, to be a heavy drinker of wine and a reckless gambler. Something had already been said of the immense amount of debt which George IV. incurred in his earlier days; of the scandalous manner in which the debt had been accumulated; and of the audacity with which appeal after appeal had been made to the House of Commons for its liquidation. The public in general were willing to let bygones be bygones, so far as the doings of the past were concerned, if only there could be some reasonable hope of an improved system in the future. Many men were inclined to regard George as a sort of Prince Hal, who might be counted on to redeem the errors of his youth the moment he was put into a position of genuine responsibility. They talked of him and of his companions as other men at a distant day might have talked of the wild Prince and Poins. Even after the Prince Regent's years had outgrown the limit of Prince Hal's wild-oats season, excuses were yet found for the Prince Regent, and admirers continued to look out for a brightening future. William Pitt, otherwise the most austere of men, drank heavily night after night; Charles Fox was a gambler; Sheridan was an irreclaimable spendthrift; and after all why should the Prince Regent be thought so much worse than they?

There was, however, a fatal levity about George IV. which prevented him from having any due sense of responsibility, even when the responsibility began to rest most heavily upon him. When he came to the throne he had outlived most of the friends whose influence he might, in political affairs at least, have had to guide him along the right path. Fox was long since dead; Sheridan had outlived him by a few years only, and the manner in which the Prince Regent had neglected Sheridan in the melancholy closing days of his ruined life became a new public

QUEEN CAROLINE.
(1768–1821.)

scandal to be added to the other scandals which had accumulated round the progress of the regency. George IV. had been married, chiefly from reasons of State, to a German Princess, Caroline of Brunswick, nearly connected with the Royal Family. The marriage turned out a most unhappy alliance in every way. George soon came to detest the wife who had been to some extent imposed on him, partly by supposed State advantages, and partly because it was hoped that she might lead him into better ways. Soon it became evident that the pair could not get on together, and in fact were nearly irreconcilable. The Queen went away to the Continent, and spent her time travelling about there. George was only too well pleased to get rid of her companionship on almost any terms, and returned to his old likings and his old free-and-easy habits. It is not necessary to enter into the details of the public scandal and the public controversy which followed. It will be enough to say that the scandal and the controversy became a subject of national importance when the new King came to be proclaimed and his Queen announced her resolve to return to England and present herself in order to take her part in the ceremonies of coronation.

The whole country divided itself into two hostile camps. The conduct of the Queen abroad had been made a subject of serious charges, which it is only right to say the majority of the English people did not believe. The general tendency of public opinion was to regard her as a calumniated and injured woman; but then again there were many who held this opinion and who nevertheless did not think it right or wise or becoming on her part that she should return and endeavour to force herself into the coronation ceremonies and create an uproar and a tumult throughout the country. Probably in the history of no modern state has there ever been so curious an exhibition of domestic tumult and scandal as was afforded by this extraordinary conflict between the King and the Queen. The Queen may be said to have been almost literally ejected from Westminster Abbey. The King became odious to the population in the streets everywhere, while many of the great municipal and public bodies gave an enthusiastic welcome to his unfortunate wife. Brougham championed the cause of the Queen in Parliament and in public, as he had already done in the legal investigations. The importance of the whole controversy and the whole outrageous scandal rests for our time in the fact that it threatened for a while to throw the English monarchical institution into utter disrepute, and that yet the monarchical institution was able to survive the crisis and wait for the coming of better days, which better days soon came. There were moments during that crisis when it almost seemed as if a common watchword, or even a common catchword, among the enemies of the Monarchy, might have brought about a popular revolution; but it must be admitted that the advisers of the English people, in all ranks and classes, except among the very wildest of brawlers, were men who persistently counselled patience, good order, and a trust in the gradual development of the constitution. The King was well known, too, to be on bad terms with his daughter, and it was understood that he had made himself a domestic tyrant over her; and this but added another to the many sources of the popular odium which directed its force against him.

In the meantime the purely political troubles went on increasing: popular demonstrations were turned into riots; riots led to prosecutions and imprisonments. The King's counsellors still could suggest nothing better than repression as a means of meeting every popular demand. The health of the King was not good. George had wasted much of his life in dissipation, and people were prematurely studying the prospect in the event of his coming to an untimely end. He had no son, and his natural successor would have seemed to be the Duke of York, his next brother, and the general opinion about the Duke of York, rightly or wrongly, was that he had all George's bad qualities and not any of George's redeeming characteristics. Satire began to deal sharply with George, and those who had charge of the law began to deal sharply with the satirists. Despite all that law could do, the newspapers would criticise the King—that is, the newspapers which appealed to the instincts of the uncourtly crowd—and the sternest measures had not been able to suppress the newspapers. George became after a while reluctant to face his loving subjects in public. He made of Brighton a sort of Caprea retreat for himself as though he were a British Tiberius, and there he hid himself away for long seasons together from the sight of the London crowd. His life had been attempted once during his Regency —by some crazy fanatic very likely; but it was not personal fear which induced George to hide himself from the sight of his people; he was only sick of seeing them—that was all.

The Peterloo Massacre, as it was called then and for long afterwards, was the most momentous event in the history of the political agitation. Massacre, indeed, is a very strong word to use, and gives the idea of a purposed and an indiscriminate slaughter, which certainly could not be taken as a calm description of what happened at Peterloo. But when the story of the event comes to be coolly told, it will be seen that there was by one means or another enough of an outrage on public rights to excuse harsh phrases in speaking of the result. There was an idea amongst many of the radicals of Manchester that it would be a good thing to start Mr. Hunt ("Orator Hunt") as what might be termed the political delegate for the district. A public meeting was called by advertisement, inviting the inhabitants to assemble on Monday, August 9, 1819, in the area near the St. Peter's Church, for the purpose of discussing and adopting a plan of parliamentary reform and choosing a representative. The local magistrates issued a proclamation declaring the meeting to be illegal, and warning the public that no one could attend it without a breach of the law. Thereupon the promoters of the meeting announced by handbill that it was not to take place, but informed the public that a requisition was to be addressed to the local authorities calling upon them to summon a meeting on the earliest possible day to consider the most effectual way of bringing about a reform in the constitution of the House of Commons. An immense number of signatures was at once attached to the requisition. This most reasonable prayer was promptly and peremptorily refused by the local authorities; and thereupon the promoters of the meeting reverted to their original purpose, and announced that the meeting would be held in St. Peter's Field on the following Monday, the 16th. The inhabitants of Manchester in general, even the working classes, seemed to have taken but little part in the preparations; but all the surrounding districts were active in sending in their representative men and their crowds of followers. Orator Hunt was to take the chair.

Early on Monday morning the crowds began to move towards the place of meeting. The more organised and strictly marshalled part of the crowd was led by twelve young men, each holding in his hand a branch of laurel, which was understood for that occasion to represent the olive of peace. There were two flags with the words "Liberty and Fraternity," "Annual Parliaments and Universal Suffrage" emblazoned on them in letters of gold. The only emblem, which even the most strained construction could describe as a revolutionary sign, was a cap of liberty borne upon a pole. The cap of liberty may no doubt have recalled to many uneasy minds the direful associations of the French Revolution; but nowhere was there the slightest evidence or even suggestion that anything more was intended than the holding of an ordinary public meeting to advocate parliamentary reform. The leaders of the demonstration publicly admonished the meeting that no insult to any one was to be permitted, and that no excuse whatever was to be given to the authorities for any attempted disturbance of the proceedings. It was distinctly enjoined that if the peace officers should attempt to arrest any man engaged in the demonstration no resistance must be offered to the action of the authorities. The committee who had charge of the meeting had laid it down as a rule that no sticks or weapons of any kind must be carried by any of those engaged in it; and this rule was very generally, although not perhaps absolutely, obeyed. A number of married women and girls took a part in the procession, moving towards the ground where the meeting was to be held. Seeing that the meeting was swelled by processions of men from the various towns and villages of the district, it is not surprising that here and there some flag or emblem was displayed which the original promoters of the demonstration would not themselves have sanctioned. There was a black flag, for instance, bearing in white letters the words "Equal Representation, or Death." This flag, however, seems to have moved the meeting, when it was noticed, more to laughter than to any other expression of emotion. By the time the hour for opening the proceedings had nearly arrived an immense mass of people was gathered together on the space which had been designed for the holding of the meeting. A more orderly assemblage, up to that moment and for some time after, could not possibly have been seen anywhere, nor when disorder did afterwards break out was it in any degree due to any action on the part of the crowd. The disorder appears to have been due altogether to the futile and mischievous terrors of the local authorities, and to the ill-advised measures which were taken to guard against any possible breach of the peace.

The magistrates had sworn in a very large number of special constables, and had called out the services of a large body of Hussars, a troop of Horse Artillery with two cannons, a regiment of infantry, and nearly eight hundred of the Cheshire Yeomanry and the Manchester Yeomanry. The military forces were all disposed in streets and lanes close to the place of meeting. At the appointed hour, Hunt, the chairman of the meeting, accompanied by a number of his friends and by a band, were seen making their way towards the appointed place. The band played the two popular national airs, "Rule Britannia" and "God save the King"; and it is stated that a large number of those attending the meeting took off their hats in token of respect for the sentiment to which the music gave expression. Mr. Hunt and his friends then mounted the platform, and it was proposed in the most quiet and orderly way that Mr. Hunt should take the chair. The motion was seconded, and carried by acclamation. Hunt thereupon advanced to address the meeting for the purpose of formally opening the proceedings. Miss Martineau's history tells us what happened then. "He had only," says the authoress, "uttered a few sentences when a confused murmur and pressure, beginning at one verge of the field and rapidly rolling onwards, brought him to a pause. The soldiers were upon the people. The magistrates, it appears, had taken it into their heads to issue a warrant for the arrest of the leading promoters of the meeting; the warrant was given into the hands of the local Chief Constable. The Chief Constable declared that he could not possibly attempt to execute the warrant without the assistance of the military; and the magistrates thereupon issued instructions to some of the commanders of the military." Up to this part of the proceedings there seems no contradiction between the account given by the promoters of the meeting and that given by the authorities. The uncertainty is as to how and why the active intervention of the soldiers began. There was, no doubt, confusion of orders and confusion of ideas. When the Yeomanry were seen advancing, Hunt, who began to be afraid that a panic might break out among those who composed the meeting, called on the people to give three cheers. The Yeomanry possibly mistook the cheers for shouts of defiance, and possibly in some way or another got it into their heads that they were ordered to advance. They did advance, at all events, waving their swords, and apparently with the intention of dispersing the meeting; but of course, as the number of the Yeomanry was comparatively small and the number of the crowd was immense, the only immediate result was that the Yeomanry got thoroughly swallowed up in the crowd and could neither advance nor retreat. Just at this moment, as luck would have it, the two squadrons of Hussars came within sight, and soon reached the verge of the crowd. Thereupon some of the magistrates, who were watching the proceedings, seemed to have thoroughly lost their heads. The impression of some of them certainly was that the Yeomanry were being overwhelmed and trampled down, and they gave to the officer in command of the Hussars the frantic order to disperse the crowd. The trumpet was sounded, and the cavalry charged the multitude. The multitude was in no condition whatever to offer any effective resistance. Even if those who composed the meeting had been prepared or inclined to resist, which they certainly were not, the manner in which they were helplessly packed together would have rendered any sort of resistance impossible. A general stampede set in; the Hussars, it is believed, in general used only the flats of their swords against the people, but as may be easily imagined in such a case, the edge of the sword was sometimes used, both by cavalry and by yeomanry. There is no reason to suppose that the soldiers acted with any deliberate and cruel purpose; but when a collision takes place between a small body of troops and a vast number of civilians whose only resistance is in the mere bulk of their crowd, the soldier striving to make his way onwards is sometimes tempted to use the edge of his weapon in order to clear a passage. In ten minutes from the first movement of the Yeomanry the meeting had broken up in utter confusion; the people had fled this way, that way, and the other; and the field was almost completely deserted, except for the bodies, some dead and some wounded, which still held the ground.

Some pitiful, pathetic evidences of a struggle also remained behind; the ground in several places was strewn with hats, caps, bonnets, coats, shawls, torn skirts, torn petticoats, shoes and slippers, which fugitives had left behind them in the stress and pressure of the flight. The actual deaths were not many, when one considers the density of the crowd and the efforts of the cavalry to clear their way through, although perhaps the very density of the crowd may have been the principal reason why the deaths were not more numerous. Only five or six persons appear to have been killed, and of these one was a special constable, and one belonged to the Manchester Yeomanry, both apparently knocked off their horses and ridden down in the confusion. About thirty wounded persons were carried to the hospitals that day, and about forty more had their wounds looked to and dressed, and were then able to return to their own homes. Others, it is believed, were wounded who did not present themselves at any hospital or infirmary. This is but natural, and is just what occurs on all similar occasions. At every great political gathering a number of men are sure to attend whose hearts are not particularly set on the objects of the popular meeting, and whose first impulse, if there be disturbance, is to endeavour to escape from being identified with any of the proceedings. Such men would be very likely, even if they had received bodily injuries at St. Peter's Field, to make as little noise about the matter as possible. They would betake themselves to their homes privately; would have their hurts seen after in their own houses; and would try to go about their ordinary occupations next day as if nothing had happened in which they had any personal concern.

It did not suit many a man in those days to give

his employer any reason for suspecting that he had been taking a part, however passive and innocent, in the business which ended in the massacre of Peterloo. Looking back now at the whole story of the day's events, it is easy enough to see that the massacre, if massacre it may still be called, was not premeditated on the part of the magistrates or on the part of the troops whom they called in so mistaken a way to their assistance. The officers in command of the troops, and the troops themselves, were, of course, entirely innocent of any desire to massacre anybody. In almost every case in the modern history of England in which the soldiers have come into collision with the populace and a calamity has been the result, the calamity has not been caused by any wanton action on the part of the soldiers or by those immediately in command of them, but by some confusion and blundering on the part of those who represented the civil authorities. In this case the magistrates undoubtedly blundered. They blundered in their notion of arresting the leaders of the crowd at the moment and on the spot, and they blundered also in the measures which they took to have the arrests accomplished. But it does not appear that they had any set desire to bring about a collision between the military force and the peaceful citizens assembled at the meeting. On the other hand, there can be no doubt that the meeting was perfectly peaceful, orderly, and legitimate. In our days, when a portion of Hyde Park has been specially set aside for the purpose of Sunday meetings in the open air, no question could arise such as that which bewildered the brains of the

Manchester magistrates; but it must be remembered that at that time the law was in a very different condition. It was the opinion of some great lawyers that the men who got up the meeting were liable to be tried on a charge of high treason. Hunt and some of his comrades were in fact put upon trial on just such a charge. Lord Eldon, who, with all his faults, was undoubtedly a great lawyer, was himself of opinion that the charge of high treason could be maintained according to law, and that also if it could be maintained according to evidence, then, but not otherwise, the magistrates were quite justified in acting as they did; for Lord Eldon distinctly laid it down that numbers constituted force, and force terror, and terror illegality. Now nothing can be more clear than this declaration, and this declaration, this construction of the law, is what makes the Peterloo meeting an epoch in English modern history. Any large public meeting whatever held in the open air with the object of bringing about a reform in any part of the constitution was an act of high treason, because numbers constituted force, and force terror, and terror illegality. It is very likely that Lord Eldon was literally correct in his application of the existing law; but the law was never heard of in such interpretation after the days of the Peterloo meeting.

The indictment against Hunt and his companions for an act of high treason broke down; the judges would not have it, and it had to be given up. The prisoners were then put upon their trial for a disturbance of the public peace, and were sentenced to various periods of imprisonment: Hunt himself spent some two years in gaol, to atone for his offence as a disturber of the public peace. The conduct of the magistrates received the formal approval of the Government, although Lord Eldon himself, in a letter which has since been published, declared that the magistrates would have been to blame if the holding of the meeting could not be shown to be an act of high treason. The important fact for the modern reader is that, according to Lord Eldon's reading of the law, any public meeting whatever which assembled in large numbers would be guilty of an act of high treason; and that even in Lord Eldon's time that interpretation was not upheld by those who had to lay down the law. Had Lord Eldon's declaration prevailed, the right of public meeting might have been denied for years and years, and any large assemblage to demand a reform of any law would be liable to forcible dispersion at the command of a civil magistrate. That position was not maintained—it thoroughly broke down; and therefore an opening was made for peaceful popular agitation, such as it might not have had for years if it had not been for the disturbance at Peterloo. Thus the poor muddle-headed magistrates who issued the order for the bringing up of the troops did more to help on the coming agitation for reform than the eloquence of Orator Hunt could ever have accomplished. It is a somewhat interesting historical fact, that on the scene of the Peterloo meeting was afterwards erected the great Free Trade Hall of Manchester, the Free Trade Hall which Richard Cobden and John Bright used as the theatre for so many a peaceful agitation, and from the platform of which nothing seditious or anarchical, or even revolutionary, was ever given forth. Thus, to adopt the words of Shakespeare, did the "whirligig of time bring about the revenges" of the Peterloo meeting.

We have thought it well to tell this story of Peterloo at some length, because of the fact that it marks the close of one part of the nineteenth century's story and the opening of another part. The calamity was, of course, in itself to be deeply lamented. But many a greater calamity has happened by accident at a public gathering, and has left behind it nothing for posterity to ponder seriously over. The fall of a platform or a gallery, the panic caused by an alarm of fire, has often had its list of killed and wounded far longer than that which belongs to the massacre of Peterloo. But nothing came, or was to come, so far as the outer public were concerned, from the results of such an accident. They carried with them no national lesson; they marked no historical crisis; they made no monument to a dead past. The Peterloo calamity was in a great measure itself an accident. But for the confusion in the minds of the magistrates, nothing might have come of it, and the next public meeting, and the next and next for many long years, might have been liable to the same interruption, the same dispersion, and the same shedding of blood. The Peterloo calamity, although in itself, to a certain extent, only an accident, yet differed from other such accidents as those we have just mentioned in the fact that it brought about a new reading of the law for practical application to the business of life in England. Of course there have been meetings prevented and meetings suppressed since that time; and, as we shall find in going on with this story, it has been left in the power of the authorities, in certain parts of the kingdom, to prohibit absolutely the holding of a public meeting in a certain place and under particular circumstances. But when such official acts are allowed and authorised, it is only where the operations of the ordinary law are supposed to be for the time suspended. England gained by the results of the Peterloo meeting the certainty that where the ordinary law still prevailed peaceful men may assemble in any number of thousands to make peaceful demands for constitutional reform, and no one shall gainsay their right of public demonstration and of free speech.

V

THE CATO STREET CONSPIRACY

ONE of the conspiracies of that season, when the air was alive with the rumours of conspiracy, was a genuine plot and a murderous plot, and therefore deserves an especial notice. This was the Cato Street Conspiracy, as it was called, a name of fear to many succeeding generations. For no short space of time a mere allusion to the Cato Street conspiracy was believed by honest Tories to be quite enough to damp the enthusiasm of the most innocent reformer. The agitation in favour of important changes in the system of government had greatly fallen off for a while. Nothing seemed to be coming of the movement; the followers grew dissatisfied, and blamed their leaders for their supposed lack of activity; despondency and disappointment were abroad among the ranks; the funds ceased to come in; and the whole organisation seemed for the moment likely to collapse. It was just then—in 1819—that the massacre of Peterloo, as it was called, and the subsequent action of the Government in reference to it, interposed to give a new stimulus to popular agitation, and to fan again into a burning flame the smouldering embers of popular passion. One of the indirect results of the Government's ill-advised action was the Cato Street Conspiracy.

The conspiracy, with all its horrors, was a small affair in itself, confined to a very limited number of conspirators, and, until its actual outbreak, as completely unknown to the vast majority of the reform agitators as it was to the vast majority of the general and unconcerned public. Indeed, it is by no means certain that there would have been any Cato Street Conspiracy at all but for the working of the abominable spy system, which was undoubtedly abetted by the officials of the Home Office. The first information of the existence of any such conspiracy was given to the Home Office by a man named Edwards, who kept a small shop at Eton. Edwards professed to have discovered a desperate plot for the assassination of the King's Ministers, and indeed it may be assumed of the King himself. The story was naturally told at once to Lord Sidmouth, the Home Secretary; and Edwards was promptly taken into the pay of the Home Office. Whether Edwards actually started the conspiracy itself it would now be impossible to say; but it is certain that he and other agents of a similar character did go about London and the country, wherever they found discontented men, and whisper to them of a tremendous plot to wreak a just vengeance on the King's Ministers and to form a starting-point for a great popular revolution. Very few men indeed were foolish enough to be persuaded to join this preposterous conspiracy; but it had from the beginning, or at all events it had after the sedulous efforts of the Government spies, the leadership of a man named Thistlewood, the very sort of man whom Fate and his own fault had marked out for such a part. Thistlewood was just a type of the creature who is found during the progress of all great popular movements, who belongs to the dregs of the agitation, and is by the hand of Nature quoted and signed to mix himself up in deeds of blood. Perhaps he was rather a crazy fanatic than an ordinary assassin; but it is certain that a spirit of private vengeance and hate urged him in his later days, much more than any desire, however wild and incoherent, for the emancipation of any downtrodden class. He had been concerned in other agitations, and had been put on his trial in one instance and acquitted. Perhaps if he had not been crazy, he might have been contented with the result; but he instantly blossomed forth into that most dangerous growth, a man with a grievance. He took the extraordinary course of sending a challenge to Lord Sidmouth. Perhaps Lord Sidmouth might have done well if he had taken no notice whatever of the challenge; but of course there are laws for the protection of the Ministers of the Crown from invitations to single combat, and Thistlewood's mock heroic performance was punished by a year's imprisonment. When his time of incarceration was over, he came out a thoroughly desperate man. He got a few creatures about him, as ignorant and as desperate as himself, and he initiated them into his plot, which was to murder the Ministers, seize on the Bank, the

Mansion House, and the Tower of London, and forthwith set up a provisional government. One of the wild fantasies among the discontented desperadoes of that time was the notion that by capturing the Bank and the Mansion House and the Tower of London they could establish a secure basis for the construction of a new system of government on the principle of "down with everything." It seems hard to think now that even men like Thistlewood and his little gang of conspirators could have believed for a moment in the possibility of such a scheme; but Thistlewood and some of his associates undoubtedly did believe in it, and they were for going to work at once, and beginning with the assassination. Some delays, however, intervened, amongst others the delay caused by the death of the King and the Duke of Kent and the uncertainty as to whether the accession of George IV. might not rid the country of the old Tory Ministers whom they hated. After a while the course of events furnished them with an opportunity which seemed to be sent by Fate for their very purpose. The man Edwards, the spy in the pay of the Home Office, obtained information for them that there was to be a Cabinet dinner on the next day at the house of Lord Harrowby. There, then, was the whole murder made easy. Some of the conspirators were to watch round Lord Harrowby's house; one was to knock at the door and send in a note while the statesmen were at dinner, and then the conspirators were to rush in a body through the open door and to massacre their enemies. So elaborate and so comically dramatic were their preparations, that some of the conspirators, it seems, came provided with bags in which to carry away the heads of Lord Sidmouth and Lord Castlereagh, the two men especially hated by Thistlewood and most of his friends.

The whole scheme turned out a grotesque failure. One of the conspiring gang gave Lord Harrowby warning of what was in preparation. Lord Harrowby showed prudence and judgment; he did not seem to take any notice of the information given to him, and the preparation for his dinner went on in the natural way, only, perhaps, a little more ostentatiously. When the hour for dining came, and the guests did not come, the conspirators who were set to watch the house took no notice of the fact. It so chanced that the Archbishop of York, who lived next door, happened to be giving a dinner party that same evening, and some of the conspirators who were set to keep watch on Lord Harrowby's house were for a time puzzled and mystified by the rapid and frequent arrival of carriages. It had been arranged that, at a certain appointed hour, the men who were to do the actual deeds of murder were to be warned that the time was arriving, and were to hasten to the spot. These men were now assembled in a stable and a room or two above it in Cato Street, off the Edgware Road, near Hyde Park. By the time the conspirators entrusted with the keeping of watch over Lord Harrowby's house had come to make up their minds that there was to be no Ministerial dinner there after all it was quite too late to give warning to their colleagues in Cato Street. These colleagues had, indeed, been warned already. The police had turned out and the soldiers had been sent for; but the soldiers were not prompt in getting to the scene of action—there had been some delay about the giving of proper orders; in fact, it was a night of mistakes on the part alike of authority and assassination. The police, without the assistance of the soldiers, endeavoured to capture the men in Cato Street; but Thistlewood and about a dozen others were able to make their escape before the soldiers came on the ground; and Thistlewood stabbed one of the policemen through the heart. When the soldiers came at last, they captured the few remaining conspirators, some nine or ten in number, with their weapons, their ammunition, and no doubt the formidable bags in which the heads of murdered Ministers were to be securely stowed away.

The *London Gazette*, the official publication, which came out next morning, contained the proclamation of a reward of £1,000 for the capture of Thistlewood. London was thrown for the time into profound consternation; the general conviction was that the Cato Street movement was but the first act of some vast revolutionary organisation, which the very fact of a first failure might render only the more ferocious and desperate. But before the alarmed citizens had time to get hold of the *Gazette* the principal conspirator was already in the hands of those whom he would himself probably have described as the minions of a despotic government. When Thistlewood escaped from the garret in Cato Street he quietly went to the house of a friend at Moorfields, and there got a night's lodging and betook himself to bed. He was still unheroically slumbering when he was aroused before eight o'clock in the morning by the emissaries of the law, and there was an end of the Cato Street Conspiracy.

That, at least, was the end of the conspiracy. The conspirators had yet to be dealt with. While they were lying in prison awaiting their trial, the King, who had been in bad health at Brighton, sent up for delivery his speech on the dissolution of Parliament on the 18th of March. It was natural, of course, that the King and his Ministers should make the very most of what had happened; but still the passage from the speech which referred to the Cato Street business was couched in such language as might have been applied to some widely-spread, vast conspiracy, gravely imperilling all the best institutions of the country, and not to the insane and fantastic plot of a handful of men, wholly unsupported by any following worth mentioning in an obscure corner of London. "Deeply as his Majesty laments that designs and practices such as those you have been recently called upon to repress should have existed in this free and happy country, we cannot sufficiently commend the prudence and firmness with which you directed your attention to the means of counteracting them." Then the speech goes on to say: "If any doubt had remained as to the nature of those principles by which the peace and happiness of the nation were so seriously menaced, or of the excesses to which they were likely to lead, the flagrant and sanguinary conspiracy which has lately been detected must open the eyes of the most incredulous, and must vindicate to the whole world the justice and expediency of those measures to which you thought it necessary to resort in defence of the constitution and the laws of the kingdom."

The fact is that the kind of measures to which the King's speech especially refers had been the very means of driving senseless men on to the crimes which the laws condemn. The manner in which the Manchester meeting was dealt with, and the protection which the law afforded to such measures, became the stimulating impulse to the crimes of which this notorious gang were guilty. It may now be taken as an axiom in the principles of government that over-repression of popular agitation inevitably leads to conspiracy.

While Thistlewood was still in prison and untried an absurd plot suddenly exploded in Scotland, a country where one might have thought there was the least possible likelihood of a merely fantastic conspiracy finding a home. This business began with the posting of proclamations—no one knew by whom they were posted — on the walls all over Glasgow, inviting the people to prepare themselves for the accomplishment of a revolution and commanding a cessation of all labour. The very fact that nobody knew who had posted the proclamations, gave them an additional importance; everybody looked to everybody else for explanation; and as no one had any explanation to give, the natural conclusion in alarmist minds was that there must be some deeply-rooted, widespread revolutionary movement going on. Nothing more terrible in the way of revolution made itself seen than the appearance of a body of armed men, who called on one of the Stirlingshire Yeomanry to surrender his weapon. The man thus challenged contrived to get back to Kylsyth, near which the armed conspirators had made their appearance, and he gave the alarm. A small body of troops was despatched, and they soon came upon the conspirators, who refused to surrender, and fired some shots, but were very soon disarmed and overpowered. Some of the conspirators were wounded, and about nineteen arrests were made, and the collision obtained the high-sounding name of the battle of Bonnymuir. Many of the unfortunate creatures who joined in this armed movement had been deluded into the belief that a great rebellion was coming on; that an army of rebels, several thousands strong, was within hail; and that they had better, for their own safety, take part at once with the forces of revolution. Nothing came of the whole business, which even in those days of severity called for no more than a light sentence on the few who were convicted and whom it was thought worth while to punish at all. After the battle of Bonnymuir, Scotland stood just where it did before. Yet the alarm that was spread through the country was as genuine and deep as it was vague and unfounded. Miss Martineau, in her "History of the Peace," has given a description, at once amusing and instructive, of the state of public feeling in many districts after the Cato Street Conspiracy. "Those," she says, "who are old enough to have a distinct recollection of those times, are astonished now to think how great was the panic which could exist without any evidence at all; how prodigious were the radical forces, which were always heard of but never seen; how every shabby and hungry-looking man met on the road was pronounced a radical; how country gentlemen, well armed, scoured the fields and lanes, and met on heaths to fight the enemy who never came; and how, even in the midst of towns, young ladies carried heavy planks and ironing boards to barricade windows, in preparation for sieges from thousands of rebels, whose footfall was long listened for in vain, through the darkness of the night." Miss. Martineau winds up her description by telling us how this imaginary state of the times was used by the alarmists as an argument against popular education, among other purposes to which it was turned, the plea being that the leaders of the radicals having circulated proclamations, must be able to write, and that this fact sufficiently proved the necessity of keeping the discontented dumb.

On the 20th of April, Thistlewood and four of his accomplices were found guilty and condemned to death. Their trial had lasted three days, and the trial only made it more and more clear that the conspiracy had been confined to a very limited number of half-crazy creatures. On the 1st of May Thistlewood and the other four were executed. The informer Edwards, who had done so much to get up the conspiracy, was never punished, and was never even brought to trial. Some attempts were made in the House of Commons to press the

Government into a prosecution of this man, and the subject, indeed, was brought forward more than once; those who pressed for the prosecution undertaking to produce ample evidence to prove his connection with the plot. The Government, however, would do nothing in the matter, and Edwards, to use a phrase of Carlyle's, "drops through the tissue of our history." It is of importance to dwell at some length on that story of the Cato Street Conspiracy. From that day to the present, what a distance we have traversed! Not for half a century has any serious charge been made against a Ministry of actually having fomented seditions by the aid of hired agents for the mere purpose of suppressing the movements and dealing heavy punishment to their leaders, and thus striking terror among the discontented, and forcing them to believe that they had better bear their sufferings in private and in silence, than bring down the vengeance of the law by any public agitation of their wrongs. It cannot be doubted by any calm observer that the policy of Lord Liverpool and Lord Sidmouth and the Six Acts were moving agents in the creation of that force of public opinion which carried the first great Reform Bill through the English Parliament. Many years after the date of Peterloo and Cato Street and the battle of Bonnymuir, Lord John Russell, who conducted that Reform Bill through the House of Commons, spoke in a passage of singular eloquence and wisdom against the futility and the folly of endeavouring to prevent agitation by the force of stern legal repression. He showed that agitation springs

ST. PAUL'S CATHEDRAL.

from grievance; that the grievance is sometimes too strong for men to bear in silence; and he quoted from the immortal passage in "Romeo and Juliet," in which the starving apothecary is asked, "Art thou so bare and full of wretchedness, and fearest to die?" is reminded that "the world is not thy friend, nor the world's law," and is therefore bidden to "be not poor, but break it." Such, indeed, would naturally have been the spirit of every appeal addressed by each Thistlewood and, lower still, by each Edwards, to the ignorant starving men whom they got to listen to them. "The world's law is not thy friend; then be not poor, but break it." The time was fast coming when thinking men in England would recognise that the cure for crime is to be found not in the suppression, but in the extension, of popular education; and that the best strength of a good constitution is found in the fact that the poorest and humblest citizen has some share in the making of the law. The more we consider the state of the laws at the time with which we have just been dealing, the greater will be our surprise, not at the amount of discontent and disorder and even crime, which was made manifest in political life, but rather at the general forbearance of the people, the integrity and discretion of most of their leaders, and the comparative quietness with which the time of trial was got over, which connected the era of order and reform with the era of repression and disorder.

The popular agitation at last took the shape of a definite movement in favour of parliamentary reform. The subject had come up again and again, in a fitful sort of way, both in Parliament and outside it, and indeed it sometimes happened that leaders of the movement appeared in Parliament at a time when there were comparatively few followers outside. Something, however, was always happening to turn men's minds away from the subject. There were foreign wars; there were dynastic troubles; there were the deaths of Sovereigns from whom nothing in the direction of reform could be hoped; and the coming up of new Sovereigns from whom something was hoped for a time, until the hope became gradually doomed to extinction.

Parliament was supposed, so far at least as the House of Commons was concerned, to be in theory a representative assembly. But, even in theory, it was for a long time the representative of the Sovereign and not of the people. The idea appeared to be that the monarch should select the places which he considered qualified for the right to send members to the House of Commons. The selections were made in the most arbitrary and haphazard fashion; were frequently made according to the personal favour of the ruler; and sometimes, even when the concession seemed given fairly enough in the first instance, the changing conditions made it wholly inapplicable and unsuitable for a future generation. The King, for example, gave the right of representation to some place of considerable importance at the time. Years went on, and owing to local circumstances the population dwindled and shrank, and at length became but a mere handful of inhabitants. Yet the right to send in representatives was left to these places all the same. It seemed to have become a sort of right and title by reason of habitude, and by reason of the fact that no one was greatly interested in challenging the authority of the King to let the representation remain wherever any of his predecessors had conferred it. The anomalies in the counties were not so great, because a county population often remains very much the same from one generation to another. But in the case of towns and villages the law of change was incessantly asserting itself, and sometimes in the most fantastic manner. A town or large village had received the right of sending representatives to the House of Commons. At the time when the right was conferred the place had a considerable population; and if we concede, as no one now would dream of conceding, the right of the Sovereign to designate suitable places for representation, the claim of this particular place may seem to be fairly established. But for some reason or other the trade of the town or village fell off; the inhabitants looked for other places in which there seemed a better chance of making a decent living; and the region became almost as deserted as Goldsmith's village. In many instances the constituency, if we may call it so, disappeared so completely that only the owner of the soil remained, and he calmly continued to send in his representative to the House of Commons. Nobody took the trouble to oppose him. It was difficult to get up any impressive agitation about that one particular anomaly, and no definite scheme of constitutional reform had yet been put together and brought before the public. One famous illustration of this condition of things became an effective argument in favour of reform at a day a little later, which we shall have to deal with more fully after a while, when a definite Reform Bill was brought forward in the House of Commons. During the debates on that question the representative of a place called Ludgershall, himself a sincere reformer, attracted much attention by the brief and effective manner in which he dealt with the question. He said: "I am the owner of Ludgershall, I am the constituency of Ludgershall, I am the representative of Ludgershall, and in each capacity I demand the disfranchisement of Ludgershall." One of the most famous places which were made conspicuous at that time was the borough of Old Sarum. Every reader who has even dipped into the history of those times must have met over and over again with allusions to such boroughs as Gatton and Old Sarum. Either case would answer as an argument for the present purpose; but we take the case of Old Sarum as being perhaps, on the whole, the more picturesque of the two. Old Sarum was a town in Wiltshire; it stood on Salisbury Plain, in the very shadow of the majestic ruins of Stonehenge, to which travellers from all ends of the earth make pilgrimage to-day. Old Sarum was authorised to send representatives to Parliament in the time of Edward I. The right of representation was renewed in the reign of Edward III., and from that time it remained until the reform agitation took distinct and practical shape in 1830; but in the meanwhile the town of Old Sarum itself had gradually disappeared. A New Sarum was arising under happier auspices a few miles away around the noble walls and spire of Salisbury Cathedral: for the New Sarum of a former day is the thriving city of Salisbury to-day. Old Sarum, however, or at least the owner of the soil, manfully stuck to the right of sending representatives to the House of Commons. Travellers who go to visit Stonehenge at the present day are often taken a little out of their direct course in order that they may be shown the few evidences that yet remain of the existence of Old Sarum, the few faint traces that are left to prove that once upon a time there was a town or village on the spot which had the right of sending men to represent it in Parliament. For years and for generations the men who sat in Parliament for the borough of Old Sarum represented nothing but the bare soil and the will of a landed proprietor.

It may at first seem incredible that such a state of things could have existed in England in the memories of men who are still living; but the actual fact is beyond dispute. In the meanwhile, new conditions of things were arising all over the country: trade and manufactures were growing here, there, and everywhere; England was gradually ceasing to be essentially an agricultural country, and was becoming a country of commerce and of manufactured goods; great towns were rising up in different parts of the island, full of life and bustle and energy, where workmen were employed by hundreds, and capital was invested to an immense amount; where crowded streets and busy shops told their story of growing and spreading prosperity. Many of these towns had no representation whatever in Parliament, while the empty spaces of Ludgershall and Old Sarum had men to speak for them in the great national chamber of debate. The fact was, that the whole parliamentary system had come to a deadlock; it was no longer practicable for the Sovereign to create constituencies wherever he thought fit; the time had passed for such an act of initiative on the part of the monarch; and on the other hand, the time had not yet come when the reform movement had become strong enough to set to work at undoing the errors of the past and introducing a rational and symmetrical system of parliamentary representation. Thus it came about that at least two-thirds of the numbers of men who sat in the House of Commons were the mere nominees of peers or great landlords. These owners of the soil, to quote the words of a modern writer, "owned their boroughs and their members, just as they owned their parks and their cattle." "Have I not a right to do what I like with my own?" was the argument of a powerful peer, even after Old Sarum had been extinguished; and in this demand he was asserting his right to nominate any one he pleased as representative of the constituency wherein he was the lord of the soil. One duke had the right of returning eleven members to Parliament; another had to be content with nominating only nine. As a matter of course, parliamentary seats were openly bought and sold. There were some cases in which the right of representation was offered for sale by public advertisement. Thus, therefore, there were two gross anomalies brought into striking contrast. On the one side of the field there were a number of absolutely empty spaces endowed with the right of sending members to the House of Commons; and on the other side there were populous and thriving towns and cities which had no legal claim whatever to parliamentary representation. It was obviously impossible that such a state of things could long continue in a country like England which was growing more every day into civilisation; but it cannot be doubted that the French Revolution had, for a time, a disheartening effect, even upon some most earnest advocates of a rational scheme of reform. Besides these outrageous anomalies, as we may fairly call them, the whole electoral system was full of the grossest abuses. When a contest took place in a borough, that is, in a borough which had any population and any voters to contest, the polling was allowed at one time to go on for six weeks, and only towards the close of the century was the time-limit reduced to fifteen days. Bribery of the grossest kind was allowed to go on without any one thinking of interfering. The cost of a severe contest was so great that nobody but a rich man, or at all events a man with rich backers, could possibly think of undertaking to stand for a constituency, no matter what his merits or his cause.

VI

GEORGE CANNING

AMONG the rising names of statesmen in the early part of the century the greatest name was undoubtedly that of George Canning. The men who have hitherto been mentioned in these pages were, for the most part, men who had won their fame before the century began, such men as Pitt and Fox and Burke. But the career of Canning belongs almost altogether to the story of the nineteenth century. Canning was the son of a literary man who was supposed to have gifts, or at all events promises, as a writer; but the highly respectable family to which he belonged regarded literature as a decidedly ungentlemanly, if not disreputable, sort of occupation; and the elder Canning was therefore edged out of the circle with a very stinted income to maintain him, and had to supplement the income by various experiments which nearly all proved to be unsuccessful. He tried to be an author, and did not succeed; he was called to the bar and endeavoured to get on as an advocate, but without success; he even tried, it is certain, to be

RIGHT HON. GEORGE CANNING, M.P.
(1770–1827.)

a wine merchant, but the public did not show any anxiety to consume his wines, and he died early, a disappointed and broken-spirited man. His widow, a very beautiful woman, was encouraged to believe that she had some talent for acting, and she accordingly, driven by the necessity of having to make a living for herself and her son, took to the stage. She played in London, but without marked success, and after a while had to be content with theatrical tours in the provinces, until at last she married an actor, and dropped out of history. Her career on the stage is chiefly to be remembered because of the obloquy it brought upon her illustrious son George Canning. While Canning was slowly rising into great reputation as an orator and a statesman, and even when he had reached the very zenith of his fame, his enemies had no worse accusation to make against him than to remind the world that he was the son of an actress. The father of Mrs. Siddons insisted at one time that his daughter must not marry an actor. Like Prospero's daughter, she broke his hest. She married Mr. Siddons, who was on the stage, and when her father remonstrated with her she smilingly excused herself on the ground that no one could regard Mr. Siddons as an actor. In the same spirit Canning might, if he had thought it fitting to notice such a taunt in any way, have contended that his mother was not an actress, either by profession or by vocation. Had Mrs. Canning been really a great actress, her son would no doubt have felt proud of her genius; but much of the sting in the taunt levelled against him was contained in the statement constantly made, that his mother was only a member of a travelling stock company. Manners have so much altered since that time that it seems hard now to understand how the enemies of a great public man could stoop to make it a charge against him, that his mother had tried to earn a living when widowed and penniless by acting on the stage. It is certain, however, that some of the most distinguished and proudly placed of Canning's political enemies did degrade themselves by constantly talking of him as the son of an actress. It is certain, too, that in his heart he bitterly resented such whispered insults. Canning, as it has been well said, was a man far too sensitive for his own happiness, and his enemies knew of his sensitiveness and practised upon it accordingly.

George Canning was born in England, and his education was undertaken by his father's brother, a rich merchant, who no doubt was anxious to repair in some measure to the son for the unkindness shown to the father, and he was sent to Eton and to Oxford. He studied for the bar; but his political gifts and his power of speech soon drew on him the attention of all who came in his way. Sheridan, who was a relative of Canning's mother, introduced him to Fox and Burke and Charles Grey. Canning cultivated assiduously, meanwhile, the art of public speaking, and he obtained a seat in Parliament in 1793. He had a singularly handsome and graceful person, fine features, and a noble forehead, and a voice which lent itself to high oratorical effort. It became a sort of fashion of speech at one time, to compliment rising young men, by declaring that their appearance was like that of Mr. Canning. Most, even of his own close associates, assumed that when Canning went into Parliament, he would at once take the position of a Whig, and rank himself with the opponents of the Tories. But Canning was at this time and for long after strongly under the influence of Pitt, to whom, indeed, he owed in great measure his first chance of obtaining a seat in the House of Commons; and also under the influence of Lord Liverpool, by whom it is said that he was first introduced to Pitt, and who had been a close friend of his at Oxford. Canning made himself conspicuous for a long time, principally as a dashing and daring assailant of the Opposition. He even stood up to Fox himself, with a courage that perhaps only youth can satisfactorily explain. If Canning had any deliberate personal purpose in the course he took, it was possibly the result of a conviction that a man cannot begin too early in striving to make an impression by any means on the House of Commons. Without genuine ability to back it, this sort of policy is sure to be a failure; but it may turn out to be a success if it is employed as a means of challenging attention to a capacity for public utterance, which might otherwise remain unnoticed, until some great opportunity came. The sensitiveness of Canning's nature might make it seem unlikely that such a man could adopt such a policy for the mere sake of making himself conspicuous in Parliament, and yet we all know that very sensitive natures do often exist with a daring ambition and an undismayed courage.

Canning was probably pursuing in the House of Commons the training to which he had subjected himself for long before in the political clubs and debating societies. In any case, he does not seem to have quite made up his mind in his early days as to the precise political opinions with which he was to identify his career. He supported Pitt, for example, in the great debates on the question of the Parliamentary Union with Ireland; but it was observed at the time that he carefully avoided committing himself to any views with regard to the Catholic claims, although the refusal of the Catholic claims was the cause of the Rebellion of 1798, and that rebellion was made the excuse for the Act of Union, which was carried in great measure by Pitt's implied promises that when the Union was carried something would be done to satisfy the Catholic demand. In fact, for a long time, Canning acted as the regular champion of Pitt in the House of Commons, and outside its doors as well. He started, in conjunction with one or two political friends, the famous *Anti-Jacobin* newspaper, a paper intended to hold up to ridicule all the doctrines of the French Revolution and of its admirers in this country. Canning was a master of brilliant political sarcasm, and there can be no doubt that the *Anti-Jacobin* became quite a power in its day. The basis of the satire was easy enough. It simply assumed that every public man who hoped for peace with France, and who talked even in the mildest way of putting any possible faith in the leaders of the French people, must be a thoroughgoing sympathiser with the sentiments of the Jacobin

GEORGE GROTE.
(1794-1871.)

Club in Paris, the club to which Danton and Robespierre belonged, must be the uncompromising enemy of the Throne, the Altar, and the aristocracy, must be a devotee of the supposed rights of man, must consider the horny-handed mechanic as the natural lord of creation, must regard education as the enemy of enlightenment, and religion as the opponent of virtue. Such were the genial assumptions on which the *Anti-Jacobin* was conducted. It must be owned that its satirical touches make bright reading, even still, and the time has yet to come, and is probably far distant, when the House of Commons is no longer to be regaled by citations from the Ballad of the Needy Knife-Grinder. Among those who co-operated with Canning in the production of the *Anti-Jacobin* was Hookham Frere, Canning's old associate, who was afterwards his parliamentary colleague and worked with him and under him in more than one Ministry.

Canning had almost avowedly entered Parliament with the view of becoming a Minister of the Crown, and his chance was not long postponed; for in the spring of 1796 he became Under-Secretary of State for Foreign Affairs. Mr. Disraeli, in one of his novels, has laid it down as a law that an Under-Secretary for Foreign Affairs whose chief is in the House of Lords, is "master of the situation." This was Canning's position, and he was undoubtedly well qualified to be master of the situation. In 1807 he became Secretary for Foreign Affairs. The splendour of his career displayed itself almost altogether in his foreign policy. The higher his position, the greater his influence, the more conspicuous became his capacity for developing a foreign policy best calculated to maintain the peace and the honour of his own country, and to discourage war and the policy that leads to war. In 1822 he was appointed Viceroy of India, and was actually on the eve of departure when the suicide of Lord Londonderry called him back to the Foreign Office.

The artificial arrangements made by the Congress of Vienna and by the Holy Alliance were already beginning to break up. This was only what any intelligent man, not to say any statesman, might have confidently anticipated; but it does not appear to have been anticipated in the least by any of the Continental statesmen who were in office, and was expected, indeed, by very few statesmen in England. The Continental Sovereigns went on as if their powers were destined to endure for ever. The faintest grumblings on the part of any of their subjects only provoked new measures of repression. The immediate result was that Spain was in a state of revolution; that along the banks of the great German rivers the young men were forming themselves into associations for the spread of liberty; that even in Vienna itself the Emperor of Austria found it hard to keep down revolt; and that in Poland the Emperor of Russia's brother, the Grand Duke Constantine, whose memory is still execrated by all patriotic Poles, was employing measures of the most atrocious severity and cruelty to crush the spirit of the kingdom; while already keen observers could see that a struggle was in preparation for the rescue of Italy from the bondage in which she had been cast by the Allied Sovereigns. There was in Germany at that time a popular dramatist named Kotzebue, some of whose plays were once very popular in England, and in adapted form and in English translation held their place on our stage for a long time, although one of them was satirised by James and Horace Smith in "The Rejected Addresses," and by Thackeray in "Pendennis." Kotzebue had held several offices under Russia, and was suspected, and indeed was known to be in the habit of sending frequent letters to the Emperor of Russia; and it was understood that the object of the letters was to direct the Emperor's attention to the movement going on among the students all over Prussia in favour of national liberty and independence. A young fanatic of the time, a Jena student, named Sand, driven to frenzy by what he had heard of Kotzebue's doings, gave with his own hand the unhappy poet a death more tragic than any described in the poet's own gloomiest drama. Sand was tried, found guilty, and sent to execution at once, and his death was made the occasion for a great popular demonstration in honour of his memory. Of course, no one could attempt to justify the murder committed by Sand; but such deeds often come as the warning to tell despotic rulers that people are growing impatient of their rule. No warning, however, was taken by the Sovereigns of the Continent, whose only idea, beyond immediate measures of repression, was to get together another European

Congress, in order to obtain sanction and support for their despotic sway. "Quick! a congress," wrote the French poet Béranger, "two—three—congresses—four, five, six congresses," and so he went on in some spirited verses to ridicule the folly of those who believed that a whole continent of peoples could be kept in order by the dictates of a meeting of crowned conspirators. It was therefore arranged that a Congress should be held at Verona, and England was invited to take part in the assembly and to send her representative to assist in guiding its councils.

Castlereagh, Lord Londonderry, would naturally have been the man chosen by England for such a purpose; but Londonderry was gone, and it was resolved to send no less a person than the Duke of Wellington in his place. The Duke was naturally the man most welcome to the Continental Sovereigns whom England could possibly send to take part in such a meeting. But for his military genius a Bourbon king would not have been on the throne of France, and the arrangements of the Congress of Vienna could never have been undertaken. The Duke of Wellington had no particular foreign policy of his own, although it must be remembered that he had wisely refrained from pledging his Government to the principles of the Holy Alliance. The Continental Sovereigns, however, believed that in the mere nomination of the Duke of Wellington they had the best guarantee of England's sympathy, approval, and support. The object for which the Congress was ostentatiously summoned was not, however, in the first instance to deal with anything but the condition of Greece, and to prevent, if possible, a war between Russia and Turkey. The Duke of Wellington, meanwhile, was informed by a French statesman that the condition of Spain would also be brought under the notice of the Congress: and the Duke of Wellington, who had just arrived in Paris, wrote home to Canning for instructions as to the course he was to pursue. Canning had been only a few days in office; but he soon made up his mind. He had never had much doubt that the Congress would seek to deal with subjects which came nearer to the hearts of most of the Sovereigns than the condition of struggling Greece.

Canning sent a reply to the Duke of Wellington, the important part of which deserves quotation as a document of the greatest moment, a proclamation of the new era which Canning was introducing into the foreign policy of England. "If," wrote Canning, "there be a determined project to interfere by force or by menace in the present struggle in Spain, so convinced are his Majesty's Government of the uselessness and danger of any such interference, so objectionable does it appear to them in principle, as well as impracticable in execution, that when the necessity arises, or, I would rather say, when the opportunity offers, I am to instruct your Grace at once frankly and peremptorily to declare that to any such interference, come what may, his Majesty will not be a party." The result of these instructions was decisive. France, through her representative, strongly argued for an interference with the Spanish Revolution by force of arms, and insisted that the condition of France herself was unsafe while only the Pyrenees divided her from the forward movement in Spain. But France might plead as she would. The instructions given by Canning to the Duke of Wellington made England's purpose too plain to be mistaken; and the baffled Sovereigns did not venture to pass any resolution in favour of any interference in Spanish affairs. Canning never had the slightest belief in the policy of governing Europe by means of Congresses. There were then two great principles in direct opposition — the principle of those who believed that a set of European kings had only to get together, and agree, in order to make their decrees a command to the civilised world; and the principle of those who believed with Canning, that the affairs of each country can only in the end be settled by its inhabitants. Here, then, was the actual parting of the ways. Canning had laid down a policy which was absolutely new at the time but which became, with some slight and fitful deviations, the settled foreign policy of England. Canning himself would undoubtedly have preferred, on the whole, to send no English representative to the Congress of Verona; but he thought so sharp a decision might be unwise at such a moment; and he believed that he could better attain his own ends by the course which he actually adopted. His own great objects were two in number. The first was to keep his own country, and if possible all other countries, at peace; and his minor and more immediate object was the practical dissolution of the Holy Alliance. It is not too much to say that George

Canning was the first Minister for England's foreign affairs who ever set up that policy of peace. His apprehensions as to the purpose of the Congress of Verona were only too soon justified. It was made known that the French army was to be sent into Spain to assist the Spanish Bourbon king in abolishing the Constitution and crushing all Spaniards who opposed his measures. The Duke of Wellington followed the instructions of his chief, as, to render him only justice, he always did: he offered his strong remonstrance; he made known the determination of England as set forth by Canning; and he withdrew from the Congress. Canning clearly saw what the course of action threatened with regard to Spain meant as regarded other countries. It was a menace to Portugal, which might be expected to join with Spain in repelling the French invasion; and it was a menace also to Spain's South American Colonies. On the 14th of April, 1823, Canning proclaimed his policy to the House of Commons. He insisted that if Portugal at her own choice and at her own risk assisted Spain in repelling the French, there was no occasion for England's intervention; but he declared that if Portugal should remain quiescent, and should nevertheless be attacked by France, that attack would bring Great Britain into the field with all her force to support the independence of her ancient and faithful ally. So far as the South American Colonies were concerned, Canning made known the policy of England in the frankest and most explicit language. "It was clear," he said, "that Spain, though claiming them as hers by right, had, in fact, lost all power and influence over them. If the expected war were to break out, and France should, as one of the events of that war, invade and take possession of any of them, so that it might become a question whether the Colonies should be ceded, and to whom; then it was of importance for the world to know that the British Government considered the separation of the South American Colonies from Spain to have been effected so completely that England would not admit for an instant any claim on the part of Spain to hand over to another Power any of those Colonies which had ceased to be under her direct and positive influence." In other words, the British Government regarded the South American Colonies as no longer belonging to Spain; but England did not feel charged with securing their independence. If, however, Spain were to proceed to the cession of any of those Colonies to some foreign Power, England would feel bound to interfere; and to such a declaration Canning added, " the British Government had at last been forced." Canning carried his policy by a triumphant majority—an overwhelming majority—in the House of Commons.

One passage of a famous speech delivered by Canning in Plymouth has already became classic in our language. It has been quoted again and again, but it will bear quotation once more, if only to show the peculiar power and grace of Canning's eloquence. Canning had been declaring that the ultimate object of his Government and of himself was to maintain the peace of the world; but he utterly repudiated the idea that "we cultivate peace either because we fear or because we are unprepared for war. The resources created by peace are the means of war. In cherishing these resources we but accumulate those means. Our present repose is no more a proof of inability to act than the state of inertness and inactivity in which I have seen those mighty masses that float in the waters above your town is a proof that they are devoid of strength and incapable of being fitted for action. You well know how soon one of these stupendous masses now reposing on their shadows in perfect stillness, how soon upon any call of patriotism or of necessity it would assume the likeness of an animated thing, instinct with life and motion, how soon it would ruffle, as it were, its swelling plumage, how quickly it would put forth all its beauty and its bravery, collect its scattered elements of strength and awaken its dormant thunder. Such as is one of those magnificent machines when springing from inaction into a display of its might—such is England herself, while apparently passive and motionless she silently concentrates the power to be put forth on an adequate occasion."

The French invaded Spain, and soon entered Madrid. The Spanish Liberal party had few resources; and had, as was natural, many differences of opinion among themselves as to the extent to which resistance might be carried, and the direction which resistance might most effectually take. Some of the Spanish leaders were summarily hanged; the Spanish King, by proclamation, abolished the Constitution, and reduced, so far as a Royal declaration could do it, the whole nation into a system of serfdom to a despotic Government. Then the French Government, flushed with such a success, actually made it known that the next step was to be the conquest, on behalf of Spain, of the insurgent Colonies in South America.

Then came the moment for Canning to back up his former declaration; and he did so with an emphasis that could not be mistaken. "It could not," he declared, "be now permitted that France should carry the war across the Atlantic, and should reconquer for Spain and hand back to Spain those Colonies over which Spain had no longer any power of her own." "We will not," said Canning, "interfere with Spain in any attempt which she may make to reconquer for herself what were once her Colonies; but we will not permit any third Power to attack or reconquer them for her." The announcement of this declaration sent a chill to the hearts of all the Ministers of the French and Spanish Bourbons. To that policy Canning adhered, as every one might have known that he would; and the first step to make it a reality was taken when it was announced to Spain that British Consuls would be sent to the South American Colonies to protect the interests of British trade and traders there. The Consuls were appointed and despatched, and this was, in point of fact, the recognition by Great Britain of the independence of the South American Colonies. Defending his policy in the House of Commons, Canning made use of some words which are never likely to be forgotten on this or the other side of the Atlantic. Contemplating Spain, he said, "such as our ancestors had known her, I resolved that if France had Spain it should not be Spain with the Indies. I called the New World into existence to redress the balance of the Old."

This was exactly what Canning had done. The famous Monroe doctrine which has sometimes been criticised very flippantly and very ignorantly in this country, was, in fact, the inspiration of George Canning. When Canning said that he had called the New World into existence to redress the balance of the Old, he was speaking not merely of the South American Colonies; he had also in his mind the great Republic of the United States. Canning had represented to President Monroe that it would be of immense advantage to the purposes of England and to the peace of the world if the United States were to announce a policy which repudiated the right of any European State to set up a Monarchical Government in any part of America without the consent of the inhabitants who were to be subjected to that Government. President Monroe welcomed the idea, and proclaimed the doctrine that America could not look on with indifference when a foreign Sovereign endeavoured to set up a kingdom of his own on American soil without the consent of the population. So curiously misunderstood has been this Monroe doctrine that writers have often asked in this country why the United States do not attempt to apply the principle to British Canada, and why they did not apply it to the Empire of Brazil. One might have thought the explanation obvious. When the United States had accomplished their independence, they found the population of Canada forming a willing and loyal colony, as they long had been, under the British Crown. When the Brazilian Colonies were changed into an Empire, the United States saw that the change was made with the perfect consent of the Brazilian population. These cases had nothing to do with the Monroe doctrine. The United States never had the least idea of asserting any right to prevent independent countries in South America or Colonies in North, from setting up or continuing any form of Government which suited their feelings and their interests. When, much later on, Louis Napoleon, then Emperor of the French, went about to set up a sort of vassal empire in Mexico with a vassal Sovereign of his own nomination, the United States, then in the midst of their tremendous Civil War, warned him again and again that such a policy could not be tolerated; and when the Civil War was over made it known to him distinctly that he must withdraw the French troops from Mexico or take the consequences. He had no choice; he withdrew his troops from Mexico; the Mexican Empire instantly vanished; and the unhappy Maximilian, the weak, well-meaning instrument of Napoleon's ambitious scheme, lost his life in consequence. But no one can suppose that the Government of the United States would have employed forcible intervention if it had merely occurred to the minds of the Mexican people to convert their President into a so-called Emperor. Canning had fulfilled his words; he had called in the New World to redress the balance of the Old.

A veteran member of the House of Lords, who was in Canning's time a Member of the House of Commons, had the good fortune to be present when Canning made his famous declaration. Many years ago he told a friend of the present writer that even while the memorable words were passing through Canning's lips there was a doubt among a considerable portion of the Members whether the words were to be a climax or an anti-climax. There was a disposition, at first, to think that Canning was likely to spoil, by what seemed to be a rhetorical conceit, the effect of his previous magnificent sentences. Some were already almost inclined to smile; but the eloquence and the earnestness of the orator swept all before them; and the concluding words of the passage became a climax as thrilling as the House of Commons has ever known, and their effect was recorded by a burst of applause again and again repeated. More than once it has happened with a great parliamentary orator that there is a moment of doubt whether one of his splendid passages is to be a success or a failure, whether he is to lift the House to his own level, or to find it fall away from him and beneath him and so miss his best effect. Something of the kind is told of a magnificent passage in one of John Bright's speeches against the policy of the Crimean War. There was a moment when some of his audience feared that his idea and the words that clothed it would pass over the heads of the Members and so be misprised; and an intense feeling of relief came when it soon was found that the arrow had gone straight to its mark in the intellects and the hearts of the listeners.

France had nothing more to say to the reconquest of the South American Colonies. Canning had proclaimed a new foreign policy for England. The Holy Alliance was an empty name thenceforth; and all that remained for the Congress of Vienna was that the world should see its work breaking up and disappearing fragment after fragment. Canning's policy, in fact, closed the era of Congresses like those of Vienna and Verona. No doubt we have had Congresses since that time, like the Congress of Paris and like the Congress of Berlin; but these have been Councils summoned together after a great war to make some arrangement as to the results of the war. They have sadly bungled their business sometimes, and have gone beyond the reasonable sphere of their duties, but they have not attempted to reconstruct the map of Europe, or to decide in arbitrary fashion for the population of any country what sort of government it is to accept at their hands. The policy of Canning gave a new direction and set up new limits for the whole foreign policy of England.

We are far from saying that England has never since that time deviated from the course of policy marked out by Canning. It would be hard, for instance, to contend that the policy which brought England into the Crimean War was in accordance with Canning's great principle. But, after all, the course of action in politics never can be as definite, never can carry with it so obvious and so inevitable a meaning, as an axiom in arithmetic or mathematics. Where political life is concerned there is always, or almost always, an opportunity for different observers to judge from a different point of view, and then we have to make allowance for the gusts of national passion which sometimes drive the State vessel from her moorings and force her at a sudden and untimely moment to brave the ocean and the rocks. But the policy of Canning is undoubtedly that which on the whole has governed English statesmanship from that time; and to which that statesmanship, though it may drift away now and then, is always certain to return. Canning did not set up any doctrine of absolute non-intervention, such as a few great Englishmen at a later period would have desired that their country should adopt. Canning would not have limited the policy of England, even if such limitation were possible at his day, to a concern simply with her own domestic affairs. He was a lover of peace; and his policy was always directed towards the maintenance of peace; but he never was in favour of the principle which, at a later day, was often contemptuously and often unjustly described as "peace at any price." There was a great deal to be said for the preaching of that doctrine, even when preached to its fullest extent; but it was never pushed in this country by such men as Cobden and Bright, for example, to the extent of an argument that England must submit to anything rather than draw a sword or fire a cannon. What men like Cobden and Bright contended for was that the policy of England ought to concern itself as a rule with the welfare of our own populations, in the first instance; and that when we intervened in the affairs of foreign countries, we were almost certain to do so with an imperfect knowledge of conditions beyond our actual experience, and we were likely to bring more harm than good, in the end, even to those whose cause we had endeavoured to benefit. Canning went quite as far as Cobden or Bright could have done, in condemning wars for mere annexation of territory or for imposing on a foreign State the political systems which we had found to work successfully at home. But Canning distinctly admitted the principle that occasions might arise when it would be necessary for England to intervene, although in a quarrel which in nowise concerned the interests of her own people, in order to defend a weak ally against wanton and cruel aggression, or to prevent a movement which we ourselves had fostered for national freedom in some foreign State from being crushed by the wanton intervention of some Power as foreign to the movement as we ourselves, and intervening on the wrong side. This, except for one or two occasional and lamentable infractions of the principle, has been the policy of England since Canning's time, a policy of general, but not absolute, non-intervention in the struggles of the European Continent. A man in private life adopts a certain resolution as a guidance for his conduct: he is perhaps led away by sudden emergency or sudden alarm, to deviate from it; but when the moment of alarm or confusion is over, he returns to it, and makes it his rule of life again, and faithfully adheres to it. Of such a man it would be only fair and just to say that he made that principle the general guidance of his life. It is so with the foreign policy of England since Canning's time. The country has on the whole adhered to Canning's policy; nor is it possible for us to think of any serious reaction against that policy being encouraged or allowed by English statesmanship. We may take it for granted that every succeeding generation will strengthen the hold of Canning's policy over the intellects and the hearts of public men in these countries and of the populations without whose support public men must cease to have control or influence. Therefore it is only uttering the merest commonplace to say that the career of Canning as Foreign Minister made a new epoch in England's foreign policy.

Many critics at the time and many readers of a later generation have sometimes found fault with Canning's speeches, on the ground that they were not inspired by any passionate enthusiasm for the cause of popular freedom. Even when he condemned the Holy Alliance and dictated the policy under which the Holy Alliance soon withered and died, he did not flame into oratorical passion over the cause of popular freedom. But it has to be remembered that with all his exalted eloquence, Canning was essentially a practical man and thoroughly understood what he could do and what he could not do. He took into full account all the difficulties that surrounded him; and he was well aware that what might be called "miracle" enthusiasm was not the soundest inspiration for English statesmanship at such a time. It would have been idle to preach up a crusade against the despotic Governments of Europe; and what Canning recommended was always a task which could be accomplished without extravagant risk to the fortunes of the State whose foreign policy was for the time in his keeping. Then, again, we have to take into consideration that there were two forces arrayed against each other at that epoch in Europe with neither of which Canning could thoroughly sympathise. There was despotism on the one side, and what has been called "the revolution" on the other. Stuart Mill, at a time very near to our own, objected strongly to such a vague phraseology as that which was in the habit of talking of "the revolution" as some definite movement. No doubt it would be much better in all writing and speaking to avoid vague and grandiose phraseology, and to define clearly in our expressions the precise idea which we mean to convey. Still, when people in Canning's day, and in a much later day, talked of the revolution, there can be no doubt that the phrase carried with it a certain meaning intelligible enough, although not capable of scientific or political definition. When men in Canning's day spoke of the revolution, they meant, and were well understood to mean, the movement against despotism, and, indeed, against all monarchy, the movement which had been engendered by despotism itself, and which threatened at one time the foundations of all monarchy. This is, in fact, the revolution which is hymned in the impassioned verses of the "Marseillaise." With that sort of revolution a man of Canning's temperament and training could have but little sympathy. Canning saw that while there were excesses on the one side there were excesses also on the other; and the memory of the French Revolution, led as a crusade by Napoleon against the monarchical systems of Europe, was a living memory in the minds of all men. Canning knew how every word he spoke as Foreign Secretary of England on a momentous occasion when peace and war were in the balance would be quoted and weighed by the advocates of the despots and by the advocates of the revolution. He had in his mind, first of all, the interests of England and the interests of peace; and he was determined not to say a word which would give to either side the hope of a support that it was not in his power to make good. He was always a cautious statesman; and his early impulses were not in any case such as would have led him into strong sympathy with the popular side of any great question. He became a supporter of Catholic Emancipation; but he was not a supporter of Popular Reform. He was cautious, even on the subject of West Indian Slavery; and he did not see his way to go any farther than the recommendation of such measures as might tend to mitigate the evils of such a system. He was, indeed, guided on all political subjects and on most social questions by his intellect and by his reason rather than by his sympathies and his emotion. He was, in fact, just the man to direct the destinies of England at a time of such terrible risk; and if he was not exactly an enthusiast, it has to be said that he lived through a crisis when enthusiasm of the romantic order was a far less valuable quality in a statesman than the judgment which sees what can be done, and the courage which maintains such a judgment in action. Thus his policy had always the advantage of being practical and of applying itself to definite ends. Others might have preached peace in language more touching; he secured peace. Others might have spoken loftier words in support of liberty; he gave liberty everywhere a chance for its existence.

Canning's attitude towards the revolution cannot be better described than in a few sentences which we quote from an admirable monograph by Mr. Frank H. Hill. "Canning," says Mr. Hill, "while welcoming national uprisings against foreign or external domination in Spain, in Greece, in South America, objected to the propaganda by pen or by sword of French principles or ideas in other countries. In theory he did not contend for the suppression of French principles in France. They might be good there, though he did not think they were; but they were bad elsewhere, because they were out of relation with the existing moral and social order, and with the traditions which have become a part, not only of the general life of the nation, but of the individual life of every one in it."

Canning was, in fact, the founder of modern Greek liberty. The rule of Turkey was becoming intolerable to the Greeks. Russia favoured and fomented the national uprising of the Greeks against their Turkish oppressors. The sympathy of these countries was given almost universally to the cause of the Greek

LORD BYRON.
(1788–1824.)

patriots. Lord Byron threw his whole soul into their cause and lost his gallant life for it, not even, as he fondly desired, dying sword in hand for Greece on a Greek battlefield, but perishing prematurely of fever among the swamps of Missolonghi. Lord Cochrane lent all the generous ardour of his energetic nature to support the Greeks in their struggle. An immense wave of popular sympathy with Greece passed over this country. Numbers of brave and brilliant young men went over from London, from all parts of Great Britain and Ireland, to help the Greeks in their struggle. Lord John Russell told the House of Commons, many years after, of the manner in which, regardless of the strict letter of international law, he and other sympathisers had openly helped to raise recruits in England for the support of the cause of Greek independence. The nation became young again in its generous sympathy with Greece. Every one it would seem who had been inspired in his youth by the reading of a Greek classic poem or the sight of a Greek statue felt himself inflamed with the passion for the Greek cause, and thousands who had never seen the Acropolis or the waves that wash the shore of Salamis, felt as if they could gladly die to drive the Turks from the sacred soil. But the struggle of the Greeks did not prosper for all that. Despite the brilliant and daring exploits of men like Bozzaris on the shore, or Kanaris with his fire-ships on the sea, there seemed little chance of driving out what Byron calls the Turkish hordes. The Greeks had not a disciplined army; they had a poor stock of munitions of war; and their resources everywhere were stinted. Russia favoured their cause; and it seemed more than probable that Russia in the last resource would send her armies to deal with the Turks. It was not the purpose of Canning that things should come to such a pass as that. His sympathies went with the cause of Greek independence; but he dreaded the risk of a European war; and he could not tell where the leadership of Russia in such a struggle might end. Therefore, he arranged and concluded a treaty in which Russia and France with England had a share, and the avowed object of which was that each of these great Powers should send some of her battleships into Greek waters, in order, if we may put it so, to see fair play—in more serious words, to take care that Turkey was not allowed to push her successes to the utter ruin of Greece. In the meantime, the principal fighting on the Turkish side was done by Ibrahim Pasha, the adopted son of Mohammed Ali, who governed Egypt as a vassal Sovereign under the Sultan of Turkey. Ibrahim Pasha was a man of something like genius and of great fighting power. The Turkish and the Egyptian navies were concentrating their forces against the Greek shores. Admiral Sir Edward Codrington was in command of the English battleships. Accidents are always happening in such cases; and somehow or other it came about that the English, French, and Russian ships of war made a swoop on the vessels of Turkey and Egypt. Now, there is a story told concerning this "untoward event," as it was afterwards described in a formal document—a story which may not be actually true, but which was in wide circulation at the time and for long after, and it is at all events too good to be lost altogether. The story was to the effect that the English Government drew up a despatch addressed to Sir Edward Codrington and recommending, according to the formal diplomatic fashion, that he should use extreme caution, not allow rashness ever to prevail over prudence, and so forth; and that this document was forwarded to Admiral Codrington by the Duke of Clarence, brother of George IV., and at that time Lord High Admiral; and that the Duke scribbled in pencil with his own hand, at the end of the despatch, the three words, "Go it, Ned!" Whether the story be true or not, it is certain that "Ned," Admiral Codrington that is, did go it, and that on the 20th of October, 1827, the Turkish and Egyptian war vessels were swept off the seas, and the Sultan had to consent to the establishment of Greece as a separate kingdom. Canning, however, did not live to see this sudden triumph of his policy; he died before the Battle of Navarino, that famous unexpected battle by which the independence of Greece was accomplished.

Canning's health had been failing of late years. He was now the constant object of the bitterest attacks made by the Tories in both Houses of Parliament. He began to feel the force of these attacks more than he would have done in his younger and more elastic years. Especially he felt the attacks when they were made in the House of Lords, and were made by men of intellect and influence—by Lord Grey, for example, who was certainly not a Tory, and who agreed in opinion with Canning on many subjects, but who lent the weight of his eloquence and his power to the Tory attacks for no other reason, apparently, than because Canning did not go so far in the liberalism of domestic politics as Lord Grey would have wished him to go. Canning, too, found a difficulty in answering Lord Grey and other assailants among the Peers, because Canning, of course, was in the House of Commons, and it was not the usage, and is not the usage still, for a member of one House to reply directly to a speech made in the other. Canning, as we have said already, was, even at the opening of his career when he was young and strong, too sensitive for his own happiness; and now, when he was sinking into years, he felt hardly able to bear up against the attacks to which he could scarcely even offer a reply. In companionship with his friend Huskisson he set to work to remodel the financial system of England. The modes in which taxation was imposed, whether by Customs Duties or Inland Duties, seemed to Canning and Huskisson to be utterly antiquated and unsuitable to modern days, cumbrous in their workings and miserably barren in their results. Up to Canning's time there was nothing that might be called a scientific principle or even a scientific theory about the imposition of Duties and the levying of taxation. There were Financial Ministers, even in Canning's time, who if on some sudden emergency a double amount of Revenue was needed, had no other idea of how to get at it than by simply doubling the amount of some particular tax. It did not seem to have occurred to them that there are limits beyond which you cannot tax any particular class of persons, and that it is always open to a citizen to do without some article altogether rather than pay too high a price for it. Either you must levy on articles of necessity or on articles of luxury. If you put too heavy a tax upon articles of luxury, most people will go without them and save their money. If you put too heavy a tax on articles of necessity, as on food, for instance, a great many people will starve and die, or else there will be an uprising in the land. Many of England's greatest troubles, after the peace that followed on the fall of Napoleon, were caused by the struggles of men whom the fear of starvation had driven into insurrection. Such systems of taxation, if pressed too far, would have helped to bring about a revolution in England, as they had already done in France. Canning and Huskisson set themselves to reduce this hideous financial chaos into order; and to establish something like a scientific principle, a sound economic principle, in the arrangements of taxation.

Canning and Huskisson were close friends; they had come into political life and into power about the same time; they both, alike, could see beyond the economics of their age; they were both alike hated and denounced because they had made their way into high ministerial office by the force of intellect and capacity, without family influence and without Royal patronage. Huskisson, as well as Canning, was commonly called an adventurer by his political enemies, simply because, although he came of a good family, he had not had aristocratic patronage or Court favour to help him on his way. These two men, then, worked together; and had many a trying time of it together. Canning's mind was made anxious, towards the close of his career, by his strong conviction that the question of Catholic Emancipation would soon have to be dealt with in a sense favourable to the Catholic claims. On this point the Duke of Wellington and he parted company. Wellington was then unbending in his opposition to the Catholic claims, although, as we shall see before long, his influence was destined to be final in securing the concession of those claims. But at the time to which we have now arrived, Wellington would not give way, and Canning would not give way. Canning pleaded powerfully in the House of Commons for the claims of the Catholics, and Wellington resigned his office as Prime Minister. There was a complete break-up of the Cabinet. Peel followed the lead of Wellington ; and a new Ministry had to be constructed. Canning was, under all the circumstances, what Lord Palmerston at a later day described himself to be, the inevitable man. Lord Eldon, of course, resigned his place as Lord Chancellor ; he was always resigning or threatening to resign ; but now that Canning appeared to be the inevitable Prime Minister, he turned the threat into a reality. Canning was entrusted by the King with the task of forming an Administration. The King was not very willing to make the offer, but there was practically no alternative ; and therefore Canning became Prime Minister. His friend Huskisson had stood by his side in the stand he made upon the Catholic claims ; and Huskisson now stood by his side in the new Administration.

Canning's tenure of office was destined to be but short. Canning and Huskisson were both in very feeble health. Huskisson was ordered abroad by his medical attendant; Canning, also, was urged to go abroad and take rest, and thus get some chance of recovering his health; but he felt that it would be impossible for him to leave his post at the time, and he resolutely determined to remain at home. His physical condition had been greatly injured not long before, by his attendance at the burial of the Duke of York. The Duke of York was the brother of the King, and stood nearest in the succession to the Throne. He had been consistently and persistently opposed to all the political principles and purposes which had guided Canning's whole Ministerial career. The nation felt but little regret at the removal of the Duke of York, whose personal defects might be excused or explained, and therefore pardoned, but whose obstinacy and perversity in public affairs were a serious obstruction to every onward and popular movement. Canning felt all the more bound to attend the funeral. The day was cold and damp in dismal January; the chapel was miserably chill and full of draughts; and the whole lengthened ceremonial sent a shock to Canning's nerves, and to his general physical system. Canning never rallied from the shock and the chill of that dreary solemnity. He struggled indeed against his approaching illness as well as he could; and even when his friend Huskisson called to see him, in order to take leave of him before going abroad, Canning bore up bravely and cheerily, and tried to make his old comrade believe that it was but a passing infirmity which kept him a prisoner in his room. Two days after Huskisson had left him, Canning removed to the Duke of Devonshire's villa at Chiswick; and a few days after his life came to an end there. He died on the 8th of August, 1827, in the very room where Charles James Fox had died not so many years before. The whole nation mourned his untimely death. Canning was but little more than fifty-seven years old when his great career came to a close.

The Duke of Wellington was then called upon to form an Administration. Some measures of political importance marked the course of the Duke's tenure of office, but for the present we are chiefly concerned with one event which might almost be said to belong to the career of Mr. Canning. There were differences of opinion in the Cabinet on many questions; and especially on those with which the name of Canning was particularly associated. Huskisson made a speech at Liverpool in addressing his constituents there, which led to a serious dispute between Wellington and himself. Huskisson told, or was reported to have told, his constituents at Liverpool that he never would have taken office under the Duke of Wellington if he had not obtained from the Duke an ample guarantee that the policy of Canning on financial and other questions was to be faithfully carried out. Wellington, with his usual bluntness, repudiated any such idea; threw contempt upon the suggestion that any gentleman to whom he had tendered office could think of insisting on any such guarantee, or making a guarantee of any kind a condition of accepting a place in the new Administration.

(Siborne's "History of the Waterloo Campaign.")

The Duke, however, suggested that what Mr. Huskisson probably did say in Liverpool was that he found in the composition of the Cabinet itself a sufficient guarantee that its measures of policy would be such as to promote the best interests of the Sovereign and the country. Huskisson hastened to explain that this was really what he did mean, and even what he did say; and the matter might not have seemed very important at the moment, but it led to important consequences. Huskisson's popularity undoubtedly suffered by this dispute; some of his best friends thought that he had not done well when he consented to take office under the Duke of Wellington, in companionship with other men who were avowed opponents of Canning's general policy. Huskisson himself began to fear that he had probably made a mistake by consenting to resume office after Canning's death. In any case, there was undoubted antagonism between the principles of Canning, which were also the principles of Huskisson, and those of the Duke of Wellington, and other members of the Cabinet. The first dispute or misunderstanding led to another dispute or misunderstanding; and Huskisson in a moment of anger sent in what the Duke of Wellington understood to be a point-blank resignation of his office. Huskisson had not, perhaps, meant so much as this; and some friends of his, and of Wellington, endeavoured to bring about their reconciliation. But the Duke held firmly or obstinately to his purpose. He insisted upon it that Huskisson had resigned his office, and that there was nothing more to be said in the matter. Therefore, there was an end of Huskisson's connection with the Wellington Administration, and the impression conveyed to many minds in the country was that he had been rudely hustled out of office, simply because he was a faithful friend and supporter of Canning; while others regarded the matter in a light less favourable to Huskisson, and insisted that he had resigned in a fit of spleen; had then endeavoured to make his excuses and get back into office again, and had met with a contemptuous and insulting refusal from the Duke of Wellington. The whole incident created a great sensation throughout the country—satirists and caricaturists made much capital out of it, and even so long after the event as the publication of Bulwer Lytton's novel, "Paul Clifford," it was found that the novelist had constructed a comic song out of the whole controversy; turned it into a quarrel about the possession of a glass of liquor, which Huskisson in a hasty moment passed to one of his comrades, thinly disguised under the name of Fighting Attie, and was vainly endeavouring to get back again, Fighting Attie contemptuously advising him to "Cease your dust," and telling him "You have resigned it, and you must." On the whole, the opinion of impartial posterity always has been that Huskisson never ought to have accepted a place in the Administration of the Duke of Wellington. No one could have questioned or doubted the purity of his motive; Huskisson joined the Wellington Administration because he sincerely believed that he might be the means of influencing the Duke and others of his colleagues in favour of more liberal measures of policy in finance and in various matters. There was some reason for such a belief. Canning had carried his point with more than one reluctant Ministry. We shall soon see how the Duke of Wellington himself came to abandon a long-maintained position, and to surrender to the policy of Catholic emancipation. But Huskisson had hardly an influence strong enough to accomplish the work which might possibly have been done by a man with the strength of Canning. Much of the good work that he had done was accomplished at Canning's impulse, and under Canning's guidance. It would have been better if he had held back at the time when death, withdrawing from office his illustrious friend and leader, had given an opportunity for the formation of a Ministry under the Duke of Wellington. Huskisson, if he had lived long enough, must have found his place, and have borne a helping hand in still further promoting the policy of his great friend and leader. But however that may be, the names of Canning and Huskisson will be always associated in the history of these countries; and the fame of the one man is as stainless as that of the other.

VII

RELIGIOUS DISABILITIES

Lord John Russell, on the 26th of February, 1828, may be said to have practically begun his great career as a Reform leader by bringing forward a motion in the House of Commons, on the subject of what were called the Test and Corporation Acts. These Acts made up a little code of legislation, intended to exclude Dissenters from any manner of State or public office, or from being elected as members of any municipal corporation. The form of exclusion was the imposition of a clumsily jumbled sort of oath, which exacted from the Dissenter, as a condition precedent to his acceptance of office, or his election to a municipal board, that he should renounce all the religious principles in which he believed, and certain religious principles, also, in which he did not believe, because the oath was a kind of double-barrelled weapon, which aimed at once at the Dissenters and the Roman Catholics. Russell's was the first serious and important attack on the whole barrier of religious test as a qualification for admission to public employment or occupa-

WESTMINSTER ABBEY.

tion. We have to throw our minds a long way back in time if we would endeavour to understand the condition of things under which it was seriously thought necessary for the safety of the State that a Dissenter should be cut off from some of the most important rights of citizenship. Indeed, it is very doubtful whether the average mind of the present day could be got without some curious process of transformation to comprehend the meaning and the motives of such a policy. There however the policy was down to the year 1828—a year which many living men can still remember—and Lord John Russell was thought by most a very bold man, and by some a very wicked man, because he had set his heart on the abolition of so antiquated, so uncivilised, and so unchristian a principle. Lord John Russell pointed out in his speech that the legislation which he condemned had, whether it were bad or good, nothing whatever to do with the actual conditions of the times at which he and his contemporaries had arrived. One can understand how the kings of a former dynasty might fancy that their thrones were made more secure by excluding Dissenters from all practical share in public affairs. That might be a very sound idea; it might be the root of a policy which deserved to be condemned by rational persons, but at least its object could be understood. The House of Hanover, however, had found in the Dissenters some of its most loyal subjects, and one might have thought it would be the business even of a selfish legislature to encourage and support them as much as possible.

Lord John Russell's speech made an undoubted effect upon the House, and was an admirable prelude to other great Reform speeches of his, which we shall have to take account of later on. The Government opposed the motion, and the opposition was led by Mr. Peel, afterwards famous as Sir Robert Peel, and, strange to say, by Mr. Huskisson. Mr. Peel in those days was still an unbending opponent of Reform in most directions; but the only explanation of Mr. Huskisson's position is probably to be found in the fact that he was strongly in favour of relieving the Catholics from their disqualifications; and he feared lest the Dissenters, if separately relieved and in the first instance, might become less earnest and less energetic on the general subject of restrictions imposed on all who did not belong to the Established Church. Despite of all opposition, Russell's motion was carried by a majority of forty-four, in a House where four hundred and thirty Members went into the Division lobbies. Many efforts were made to amend the Bill brought in by Lord John Russell as the result of the passing of his resolution; but they did not make any serious difference in the proposed reform, and the measure was carried through the Commons, and sent up to the House of Lords. Some of the Archbishops and the Bishops in that House were so liberal in the construction of their duties as actually to support the Bill, much to the horror of Lord Eldon, who must surely have thought at the time that the world was coming to an end. Lord Eldon bemoaned the national calamity that such a Bill should have been introduced by the Government;

but he added, "what is most calamitous of all, is that the Archbishops and several of the Bishops are also against us. What they can mean," he declared, "they best know, for nobody else can tell; and sooner or later, perhaps in this very year, almost certainly in the next, the concessions to the Dissenters must be followed by the like concessions to the Roman Catholics."

Lord Eldon was quite right. To do him justice, his worst bigotry never utterly dimmed his clearness of vision, and he knew well what some, even of the supporters of the Bill, did not quite know, that it would be impossible to strike the shackles off the limbs of the Dissenters, and composedly leave them for ever on the limbs of the Roman Catholics. There is always something interesting to the living student of history in the spoken and written utterances of Lord Eldon on such a subject. First it is interesting, as a mere matter of curiosity, for a reader of the present day to be brought into contact with so complete and all-round a bigot as Lord Eldon; and next it is interesting to see how Lord Eldon never failed to understand the uselessness and the futility of his own bigotry. He never lulled himself for a moment, as so many of his contemporary bigots did, into the fond belief that he could stem the tide of liberal reform in religious and political affairs. He performed his duty with the full conviction that the performance would not have the slightest effect in keeping back the movement which he strove to resist. If it were not something too whimsical to compare the tough old Tory with a pretty and winsome maiden, it might be said that Lord Eldon was now performing a part like that of the high-born Scottish damsel, renowned in the history of Scotland, who made of her slender arm a bolt to hold the King's door against the fierce conspirators who were battering from the outside, well knowing that that frail barricade must be splintered and smashed without delaying for half a moment the entrance of the traitors. Yet Lord Eldon might have been comforted if he could only have known that although the Bill was destined to pass, it would, at all events, be made in itself an instrument to maintain for a little longer a system of intolerance which was probably not in Lord Eldon's mind when he was denouncing the admission of Dissenters to civil office, and foretelling, as a consequence, the admission of Roman Catholics. One of the Bishops proposed to add to the new form of oath certain words proclaiming a belief in our common Christianity. Accordingly, after much debate, the words were inserted "on the true faith of a Christian." One of the peers who bore an honoured name, Lord Holland, entered his protest on the books of the House against this so-called amendment. It should be explained that by ancient usage, a Member of the House of Peers has the right of recording on the books of that House his protest against any particular decision, and his reasons for protesting ; while no such custom prevails, or right exists, in the House of Commons. The protests of the Lords, therefore, form an interesting and important part of our parliamentary history ; they note the growth, very slow growth indeed, of sound political principles, even in the House of Lords. A Member of the House of Commons, now some years dead, Mr. Thorold Rogers, compiled a little work on the subject, which is well worth the consideration of all students of our history. We may quote here the words in which Lord Holland explains and justifies his protest. "Because the introduction of the words, 'upon the true faith of a Christian,' implies an opinion in which I cannot conscientiously concur—namely, that a particular faith in matters of religion is necessary to the proper discharge of duties purely political or temporal." The amendment adopted by the Lords was accepted by the Commons, and in the beginning of May the whole measure received the Royal assent. It will be remembered that the words, "on the true faith of a Christian," were used until a comparatively recent date as the means of shutting out the whole of our Jewish fellow-citizens from the right of representation in the House of Commons. Had Lord John Russell's measure been carried as it was designed by him, England would have been spared Session after Session an ignoble and futile struggle against the admission of Jews to Parliament. Until the final struggle within the memories of most of us, a Jew might exercise, and could not be kept from exercising, the highest influence in public affairs; but he could not become a Member of the House of Commons. He might advance money to princes and kings; he might finance a foreign policy, and raise loans to supply the munitions of war—he was always welcome to perform services like these; but he could not pass the Bar of the Representative Chamber; he could not open his mouth in that Chamber or go into the lobby, either with the Ayes or with the Noes. Lord John Russell, however, had struck his first blow against the policy of sectarian exclusion, and the portals were, as a result, to be thrown open in the end to all duly elected comers, without distinction of creed or class.

The agitation for the emancipation of Roman Catholics in Great Britain and Ireland began with renewed force towards the end of the reign of George III. It has been already shown in these pages that George III. had resisted every effort made by William Pitt to introduce any measure for the relief of Roman Catholics from the unjust, ignoble, and absurd penalties imposed on them by English legislation. With the coming of George IV. to the throne new hopes were excited in the minds of the Catholics, especially of the Irish Catholics, because of the liberal tendencies which George had shown at one time, and because of his association with Fox and Sheridan and other friends of religious liberty all over the world. It seems extraordinary, now, to think that at a period so near to our own, a Roman Catholic was still prevented from sitting in Parliament, and that great statesmen were found who approved of such an exclusion. When George IV. came to the throne, the feeling of Ireland was strongly in his favour, because Irishmen fully believed that he had come to do justice to them and to their hopes. When George went over to Ireland, he was received, wherever he presented himself, with impassioned outbursts of popular welcome. An obelisk still marks the spot, on the shore of Dublin Bay, where George put his foot for the first time on Irish soil. The village where he landed was then called Dunleary, but the local authorities in a transport of gratitude—that gratitude, no doubt, which was once humorously described as "a lively expectation of favours to come"—declared that the old name should be known no more, and that the place should thenceforward be called Kingstown; and Kingstown it is to the present day.

George IV., however, soon disappointed all the hopes which had been formed by O'Connell, by Thomas Moore, and by the leaders of the Catholics all over the country. At length it became quite apparent that the King had not the least intention of encouraging any proposal for the relief of the Roman Catholics; and an agitation set in which became before long too powerful for any combination of official statesmen to resist. The Catholic Association formed a body called into existence for the purpose of stirring up and guiding the agitation, and Daniel O'Connell became the recognised head of the movement. O'Connell knew that many of the leading intellects of England were on the side of Catholic emancipation. Canning was well known to have been in its favour; and indeed it was the only Liberal measure in domestic policy with which Canning's sympathies entirely went. Peel was too great a statesman to be set down by any one as having a mind impervious to the obvious justice and the inevitable claims of the policy of religious liberty.

Those who have studied the published letters of Sir Robert Peel must have followed with much interest the revelations they contain of the gradual working of Peel's mind towards the enlightened policy which he afterwards adopted. There are not many passages in English history which enable one thus to see into the mind and heart of a great statesman, at a supreme crisis in national policy, which allow us to observe how day after day, and by event after event, a mind like that of Peel is won from all early prejudices and traditions, and is brought to recognise the truth of a great principle in political affairs. O'Connell soon became a commanding power in Ireland. Between him and Sir Robert Peel there was not then, or at any other time, anything like personal or political sympathy; but Peel could not help recognising the force of the new and great power which was arising in political life. O'Connell was peculiarly adapted by nature for the part he had to play. He was a born agitator and leader of agitations; he was a popular orator of the highest order. Nature had given him a commanding presence; he was a man of colossal stature and colossal energy; and he had a voice which enraptured every listener. Long after O'Connell's death, Mr. Disraeli, who had no personal or political sympathy with the great Irish leader, wrote of Sir Robert Peel, that Peel's was the finest voice to which the House of Commons in his time had ever listened, "except indeed, the thrilling tones of O'Connell." The first Lord Lytton in his poem, "St. Stephen's," breaks into positive raptures over the power and the music of O'Connell's voice, and over O'Connell's eloquence in addressing a vast out-of-door meeting. Even in the House of Commons, which he entered after he had accomplished his greatest triumph, and where he found an audience for the most part bitterly hostile, O'Connell conquered that audience, and compelled those to admire the orator who most cordially disliked the political leader. O'Connell was for a long time hated in England, at least by the anti-reformers of England, more bitterly than any other man of his day. Some of the great London papers seemed to have lost all sense of justice and even of decency when they came to criticise him. He had been a foremost advocate at the Irish Bar, and was making a positive fortune by his practice. In order to devote himself to the Catholic agitation he had given up his work at the Law Courts, and reduced himself from the position of a man earning a large annual income to the position of a man earning no income at all. Yet these newspapers denounced him and calumniated him as if he had been an impostor who got up the whole Catholic agitation as a means of putting money in his own pocket. The Irish people raised a fund to enable him to live, and to enable him also to carry on the agitation; and the leading London journal forthwith designated him "the big beggar-man." The Irish people had before that time raised a national fund for Grattan, and no Englishman ever founded on that fact any question as to Grattan's unselfishness and sincerity. The English Free Trade party, in days nearer to our own, raised a very large fund to enable Richard Cobden to maintain himself while carrying on the Anti-Corn Law movement; and even Cobden's most bitter enemies never described him as a beggar-man.

O'Connell soon raised himself into a position of something like dictatorship over the vast majority of the Irish people. His genius was peculiarly Celtic— he had the imagination, the suffusion of the poetic, the rich humour, and the fitful changes of expression which belong to the temperament of the Celt. He could move his audiences to tears or laughter, to passion or to good humour just as he willed. Then he had all the astuteness of the lawyer, all the inexhaustible resources of the born politician to aid him in carrying on the work to which he had devoted his heart and soul. He soon entered into an alliance, more or less avowed, with the leaders of the Democratic party in England and in Scotland. His sympathies went with every movement for religious equality and for political reform; and we shall have occasion to see, a little later on, how thoroughly he was in tone and in harmony with the most advanced of the English Liberals. The English Liberals soon found that he was a man who had to be reckoned with; and they soon found, too, that he was a man who could be trusted to co-operate faithfully with them in the advocacy of every great reform. He had been one of those who cordially welcomed George IV. on the occasion of that memorable visit to Ireland, and it was some time before he could thoroughly rouse himself to face the fact that George cared nothing about Catholic Emancipation, and

DANIEL O'CONNELL, M.P.
(1775-1847.)

just as little about Ireland. A sudden chance, almost an accident, gave O'Connell an opportunity of testing his power in his own country. One of the members of the Government resigned his position as head of the Board of Trade, and another man was appointed to the office. The new-comer, Mr. Vesey Fitzgerald, who represented an Irish constituency, had to go back to Clare and be re-elected, before he could enter on the duties of his new position. O'Connell seized the opportunity and boldly came forward as a rival for the suffrages of the electors of Clare, such electors as there were then under the old-fashioned system of restrictions. O'Connell, as a Roman Catholic, was excluded by law from taking a seat in the House of Commons. His bold step in coming forward as candidate created the wildest excitement all over the country. Many, even of those who thoroughly sympathised with his cause, were convinced that the step he had taken was too daring an outrage upon existing law, to do anything but harm to the movement for Catholic Emancipation. From all sides, except alone from the side of his ardent followers, he received warnings; but the warnings were happily unheeded. O'Connell went to the poll, and was elected member for Clare by an overwhelming majority of votes. It was one thing, however, to be elected for Clare, and quite another thing to take his seat in the House of Commons. The oath which was then administered to all new members who came to take their seats, was one which no Roman Catholic could possibly have accepted, and one which was framed expressly with the purpose of excluding Roman Catholics from any part in the deliberations of Parliament. The oath was tendered to O'Connell, and of course he could not accept it, and he stated his reasons, and was ordered to withdraw. He did withdraw; and he left the House knowing full well that the time could not be far distant when he and other Catholics, legally elected as he had been, would find a seat in that House unchallenged by any prohibitory test. O'Connell went back to Clare, and was re-elected without opposition.

Perhaps the most interesting study for the reader of the history of those days is the manner in which the development of the whole controversy worked upon the mind of Sir Robert Peel. As every one knows, Peel had been for long years a steady opponent of the Catholic claims. He was born and brought up in an atmosphere of the most dense and rigid Toryism. He was always too enlightened a man to persuade himself into the belief that the Catholics ought to be kept in a position of political inequality and degradation, merely because he and his friends did not approve of the Roman Catholic religion. Peel, however, had succeeded in persuading himself that to admit the Catholics to political equality would only open the way for them to damage or destroy the State Church in England and in Ireland. Now as regarded the State Church in Ireland, Peel was unquestionably a man of foresight. The moment the Catholics were admitted to full political equality, the moment they could send representatives to speak up for their cause in the

House of Commons, that moment the State Church in Ireland was foredoomed. Peel could not see that the doom of the State Church in Ireland was no reason for the doom of the State Church in England; in fact, that every reasonable argument in favour of the English Establishment was an argument against the Irish State Church. The Irish Church was a Church of a miserably small minority; a Church of which the threshold was never crossed, never would be crossed, by any of the vast majority of the Irish people. Five-sixths, at least, of the Irish population were Catholics, whom the whole system of the penal laws had utterly failed to compel to any recognition of the Irish State Church. It would have been obvious, therefore, to a man of less foresight than Peel, that to give the Catholics in Ireland the full right of vote and representation would be to speak the doom of the Irish Church. The doom might be delayed, as it was in fact delayed until our own times; but it was certain to come. What Peel failed to understand was that the English Church system rested on a totally different basis; and that it was so far acknowledged and supported as a Church by the great majority of the English people. Therefore, for many years, Peel persuaded himself that he could not in conscience, as a Protestant, yield to the Catholic claims. Such, as we have seen, was the position taken up by George III., and for a time, taken up and stubbornly maintained by George IV. But then Peel's was a very different intellect from that of George III. or George IV. Peel was a thorough statesman, and he could not shut his eyes to facts, or disguise from himself the meaning of those facts, as it showed itself to all intelligent and enlightened minds. It began to be gradually borne in upon him that the concession of the Catholic claims was inevitable. The Marquis of Wellesley, elder brother of the Duke of Wellington, had been appointed Lord-Lieutenant of Ireland, partly because he was supposed to be the sort of man who could make head against the Catholic claims; and the Marquis of Wellesley had not been long in Dublin Castle before he became convinced that the claims of the Catholics would have to be conceded. He resigned his post as Irish Viceroy when the Duke of Wellington, on taking the office of Prime Minister, announced that Catholic Emancipation was not to be a Cabinet measure. He was succeeded in the Irish Viceroyalty by the Marquis of Anglesey, who had been a distinguished soldier in the wars against Napoleon, and rendered brilliant services on the field of Waterloo. Lord Anglesey was known to be opposed to Catholic Emancipation, and had actually spoken vehemently against that and all other Irish claims when he was a member of Parliament. But Lord Anglesey had not been long in office before he, too, recognised the absolute necessity of conceding political equality to the Irish Catholics. The question came up in a manner which compelled the Government to give immediate attention to it. In the vehemence of the popular commotion caused by O'Connell and the Catholic Association, an Act had been passed for a limited number of years for the suppression of the Catholic Association and all other unlawful associations in Ireland, thus putting on a show of fair play by including the operations of Orange societies within its scope, but really directed, and with the knowledge of every one, against O'Connell and the Catholics. This Act was shortly about to expire, and the question was whether it could be renewed, and what was to happen if it were not renewed. Lord Anglesey pressed these questions on the notice of the Government, announcing his conviction that the Catholics could not much longer be kept in subjection without civil disturbance, and declaring himself to be an advocate of peace, not indeed at any price, but certainly at the price of Catholic Emancipation. All this must have profoundly impressed the mind of Peel.

In the early part of 1828 an important resolution was brought forward in the House of Commons by Sir Francis Burdett, then in the front of the Reform movement, calling on the House to consider the state of the laws affecting the King's Roman Catholic subjects in Great Britain and Ireland "with a view to such a final and conciliatory settlement as may be conducive to the peace and strength of the United Kingdom, to the stability of the Protestant Establishment, and to the general satisfaction and concord of all classes of His Majesty's subjects." This resolution was actually carried by two hundred and seventy-two votes against two hundred and sixty-six. Peel was particularly impressed by one passage in the speech of Brougham in support of the resolution. Brougham's observation was that no single member of those who had opposed the motion of Sir Francis Burdett had affirmed the proposition that things could remain as they were, and that it was impossible to conceal or deny the great progress which this question had made in Parliament and the much greater progress which it had made out of doors. One can easily understand how a statement like this, the truth of which could not be challenged for a moment, must have helped to bring conviction to the mind of Peel. Of course a mere fanatic or a mere dreamer would not have been moved from a previous opinion by any such consideration. What would it be to him if the majority of the House of Commons, if the majority of the public out of doors, were opposed to his own personal opinions on the subject? "So much the worse," our fanatic or dreamer would say, "for the House of Commons and for the public, in the end; they will find out that I am in the right and that they are in the wrong; and they will have to put up with the results of their obstinacy." But of course Peel was neither a fanatic nor a dreamer; he was above all things a clear-headed practical statesman, and had no inclination whatever to fight against the stars in their courses, especially when he began to have the conviction brought home to him that the stars in their courses were fighting on the right side. Peel not merely counted but weighed the votes in that debate. He observes in one of his letters that "without depreciating the abilities or authority of those who concurred with me in resisting the motion"—for it has to be observed that Peel as yet had not seen his way to vote for the motion—any one acquainted with the House of Commons at that time would readily admit that the great preponderance of talent and of influence on the future decisions of the House of Commons was ranged on the other side. The Government at all events went so far, instructed by events, as to give up the idea of asking Parliament for a renewal of the Act against the Catholic Association. Of course Peel followed closely the events preceding the Clare election and the result of the vote. He knew that Vesey Fitzgerald, the defeated candidate for Clare, was one of the most popular men in Ireland. Fitzgerald had represented Clare for many years, and had always supported by his speeches and his votes the claim of the Catholics for political emancipation. He was a son of the man who fought stoutly against the Act of Union by the side of Henry Grattan and Sir John Parnell. Certainly a better man could not have been found to contest on the Government side the candidature of O'Connell; yet he was hopelessly defeated. In fact a great constitutional crisis had arisen, and even Lord Eldon unbent so far as to admit that the result of the Clare election must be to bring the Catholic question to a conclusion before long, a conclusion of which he highly disapproved, as was only natural for him, but which he felt it was not in the power of himself or any other man or set of men to prevent. When a man like Lord Eldon could thus far stifle his most inveterate prejudices and passions and could see the results which were destined to come, it is not likely indeed that a man of Peel's intellect and clear-sightedness could close his eyes against the lessons of the crisis.

In the meanwhile Peel was continually pressed by Lord Anglesey to come to some decision on the subject. There was a tremendous difficulty in front, and Anglesey saw but one way out of it. What he felt is well expressed in a letter which he wrote in order that it might be formally submitted to the Duke of Wellington and to Sir Robert Peel. In speaking of the Catholics he said: "I believe their success inevitable, and that no power under heaven can arrest its progress. There may be rebellion, you may put to death thousands, you may suppress it, but it will only be to put off the day of compromise." Lord Anglesey over and over again in reply to the arguments of those who were accustomed to ask, as Lord Melbourne later on used to ask, "Can't you let things stay as they are?" points out that as far as the Catholic claims are concerned things will not stay as they are, that no power of horse, foot and artillery can compel them to stay as they are. In Lord Anglesey's opinion rebellion was certain to come if the Catholic claims were thrust aside, and he further believed that even if one rebellion were put down another and another would come on till Catholic Emancipation had been granted. At one crisis of the movement we find Peel, from his published correspondence, asking himself the question which we record here at full length because of its momentous nature, and because also of the light it throws on the statesmanlike and practical manner in which the mind of Peel grasped the whole situation, and the kind of dramatic instinct which belonged to him, and without which there can be no genuine statesmanship, the dramatic instinct which enables a man to enter into the feelings of his opponents, and to realise the meaning of their cause as it presents itself to them. Peel asks himself "whether it may not be possible that the fever of political and religious excitement which was quickening the pulse and fluttering the bosom of the whole Catholic population—which had inspired the serf of Clare with the resolution and the energy of a free man—which had in the twinkling of an eye made all considerations of personal gratitude, ancient family connection, local preferences, the fear of worldly injury, the hope of worldly advantage subordinate to the one absorbing sense of religious obligation and public duty whether, I say, it might not be possible that the contagion of that feverish excitement might spread beyond the barriers which under ordinary circumstances the habits of military obedience and the strictness of military discipline oppose to all such external influences?" It need hardly be said that the British army was at this time, as it is now, largely recruited from the Irish Catholic population, and was it absolutely certain that the Irish Catholics in uniform could be relied upon at such a crisis to shoot down their fellow-Irishmen and fellow-Catholics, who were engaged in the defence of the Irish and the Catholic cause? Peel shook his head over this difficulty, and felt satisfied that only a man in a fool's paradise could feel quite sure that Irishmen in the army could all be relied upon for such a sacrifice of their religion and their country. Peel, of course, was not a soldier, but Lord Anglesey, who was a brilliant soldier of long experience, was even more doubtful than Peel as to the possibility of keeping the Irish Catholic soldiers under the British flag if an insurrection, caused by the rejection of the Catholic claims, were to break out in Ireland. At a time much later than that of Peel we have seen how, in the war between France and Austria, large numbers of Venetian soldiers in the Austrian service crossed over on the very battle-field to the ranks of France rather than fight for those who held them in subjection, against those who promised to set them free; and in that case there was no religious question to intensify the patriotic fervour of the Venetian soldier. When we read the words in which Peel speaks of O'Connell's candidature for Clare as having inspired the serf of Clare with the resolution and the energy of a free man, we must remember, in order to appreciate the firm composure of Peel's judgment, that it was the fashion of nearly all Tory politicians at the time to treat O'Connell and his agitation with utter contempt. The theory, even of many enlightened Englishmen just then, was that O'Connell was simply a self-seeking and noisy impostor who had succeeded somehow in setting the whole Catholic population in Ireland mad.

This sort of idea is indeed a favourite theory amongst men of strong prejudice and weak intellect when any great constitutional crisis arises which is distasteful to them and to their friends. It had been applied to the French Revolution until the revolution became too strong to be disposed of any longer by the theory of an insane population and half a dozen

RIGHT HON. SIR ROBERT PEEL, BART., M.P.
(1788 1850.)

self-seeking and crafty demagogues. Peel's intellect was not one which could be long deluded by the demagogue and the Bedlamite theory. What was it, he asked himself, which had inspired the serf of Clare with the resolution and the energy of a free man? Was it not the serf's conviction that he had a great national and religious cause to fight for, and if needs were to die for? Peel's mind was gradually and rapidly coming round to Lord Anglesey's view of the crisis; and it was not long before he had reached the settled conviction that Parliament must grant Catholic Emancipation. Here, again, we have to observe how different was the character of Peel from that of other statesmen who had at other times anything like a similar crisis to encounter. It has happened more than once in English history since the days of the Catholic question, that a statesman having combated successfully a certain political movement for session after session has at last been forced to the conclusion that the movement was growing too strong to be resisted much longer, and that as it was destined to be successful he might as well have the honour of its success as any other. There is an instance in modern English history of a statesman who having thus been forced to make up his mind to the inevitable success of a movement which he had hitherto opposed with all his might and main, came to think that after all he might as well take advantage of the crisis by putting himself at the head of the movement, and carrying it to a parliamentary success. Peel never could be a statesman of this light-minded order; he now felt convinced that

Catholic Emancipation must be carried, and his one great concern was in the question, Who is the best man to carry it? He decided that for many reasons he himself was not that man. He was strongly of opinion that the difficulties in the way of passing such a measure through the House of Commons and through the House of Lords would be enormously increased if the measure were to be introduced by one on whom the Tories of both Houses had long relied as the strongest bulwark against the Catholic agitation. He had many personal objections to the undertaking of a task which would of necessity compel him to enter into negotiations with the Catholic leaders and to discuss possible compromises; but these personal objections would have counted for little with him if he could persuade himself that he was the most suitable person to conduct such negotiations, and to consider suggested compromises. He took it for granted that he must, during his long career as a Tory statesman, have aroused a hostile feeling against him in the minds of the Irish Catholic leaders, and he firmly believed that a measure brought in by some Minister more popular in Ireland would be welcomed with more gratefulness and more cordiality by O'Connell and his associates in the Catholic movement. Peel's intention was, therefore, to resign his office, and leave some statesman who might be considered better fitted for the task to bring in the measure for Catholic Emancipation. Peel's own idea was that Earl Grey, who had always been an advocate of civil and religious liberty, would be the best man whom the King could invite to form a Government and to deal with the Catholic claims. But before this stage of the arrangements could be reached Peel had to gain over the Duke of Wellington to his side and persuade the Duke to conquer the King's opposition. It was difficult enough to persuade the Duke of Wellington, who had so lately announced that nothing was to be done for the Catholic claims; but Peel succeeded in bringing Wellington to listen to reason. The difficulty he had was all the greater because Lord Anglesey had lately been dismissed from his office as Lord-Lieutenant of Ireland, on the ground that he had shown a want of discretion in talking too freely in Ireland about differences in the Cabinet on the subject of the Catholic claims. We may safely assume that Lord Anglesey was dismissed from office because the King could not put up any longer with his strenuous recommendations that those claims should be taken into consideration. In any case, Lord Anglesey's dismissal must have seemed to Peel to make the task of winning over the Duke of Wellington more difficult. But the Duke was won over before long. The truth was that the Duke had an absolute faith in Peel's judgment and statesmanship, and when Peel made up his mind the Duke felt himself bound to make up his mind in the same way. The Duke's position then and on other occasions was perfectly simple. If he had been commanding an army in a foreign and a difficult country he would have accepted the services of a guide who knew the place, and would have followed the teachings of the guide when in order to reach a certain spot he was advised to go this way rather than that. In the same spirit he accepted the guidance of Peel. "Peel," he said to himself, "knows all about this political question; I do not, and I am quite certain that the King does not; therefore I am bound to follow Peel's guidance and to do all that I can to get the King to follow it as well." One thing the Duke certainly did know all about, and was satisfied that he did know all about it: he knew perfectly well that he could not possibly get on without Peel, and therefore he implored and he insisted that Peel must give up all idea of resigning his office and must not leave him, the Duke, all alone to face in bewilderment the difficulties of the crisis. He made it a question of old comradeship, and put it to Peel not to desert his comrade at a moment of such peril. Thus adjured, Peel could not possibly press his resolve, and he therefore consented to stand by the Duke so long as the Duke would stand by him.

That difficulty at all events was over. Indeed it became apparent that the idea of prevailing on the King to invoke the services of Lord Grey was absolutely out of the question. The King detested Lord Grey. George IV. had been accustomed to Ministers and to followers who yielded to him and flattered him and nourished his self-love and his absurd pride in his own judgment. Lord Grey was a cold, stern, unbending man, who acted only on the dictates of his reason and his conscience, and into whose mind it never entered that he was bound to cajole his Sovereign by any sort of flattery or semblance of intellectual deference. Indeed it was strongly believed by many at the time that one of the King's chief objections to Catholic Emancipation was found in the fact that Grey was in favour of the principle, and that Grey had again and again proved unyielding on questions of policy. George believed that the judgment of the Sovereign was entitled to exact implicit obedience from any Minister. Therefore Peel consented to hold his place in the Duke of Wellington's Ministry, and the Duke agreed to approach the King and endeavour to make him listen to reason. The Duke soon found that the task was even more difficult than he had supposed it to be. George III. had resisted Pitt, but, to do him justice, out of conscientious motives, however perverted the principle of conscience might have been, simply because he believed that it was an offence against the religion of the State for an English Sovereign to allow religious equality to those who professed the faith of Rome. If George III. could have been persuaded by the tongues of men or of angels that to approve of Catholic Emancipation would not have been to break his coronation oath, he might have consented to the policy of Pitt and of Canning. But with George IV. there were mixed motives. He professed to feel the conscientious objection, but there can be no doubt that he felt still more strongly the blow to his foolish self-conceit and his absurd idea of his own personal dignity which would have to be borne if he were to consent to give way to any one on such a question. George had lately said, on more than one occasion, that if his subjects did not like a Protestant king they could find a Catholic king in the Duke of Clarence, whom, for some reason or other, George chose to regard as a devoted advocate of the Catholic claims. George met the Duke of Wellington in the same spirit, and after many ineffectual disputations Wellington and Peel were forced to the conclusion that it would be impossible to obtain the King's consent, point blank, to any measure of Catholic Emancipation. They therefore devised a little plan by which to get round their obstinate sovereign. They obtained leave to draw up and submit to the King for his consideration, a memorandum containing their views of a policy to be adopted with regard to the consideration of the whole Irish question, without any special reference to Catholic Emancipation. This scheme did indeed include Catholic Emancipation, but that was only one subject among others, and it was fondly hoped that the King might be thus cajoled into allowing the whole scheme to pass without objection, seeing that it no longer rested on Catholic Emancipation alone. The King yielded so far as to consent to have the scheme submitted to him, but distinctly declared that he would not pledge himself to give it a favourable consideration. Time was pressing; Peel had already given formal notice in the House of Commons that on a certain day near at hand he would call attention to the whole subject of the disabilities imposed on Roman Catholics. On the day just before that which Peel had appointed for his statement in the House, he was summoned, with the Duke of Wellington and the Lord Chancellor, to attend the Sovereign. Then the King bluntly declared that he would not tolerate any alteration in the Oath of Supremacy. There was a long argument on the subject. The Duke and Peel and the Lord Chancellor, Lord Lyndhurst, endeavoured to get the King to understand that without some alteration in the Oath of Supremacy it would be perfectly impossible to do anything for the Catholics, because the Oath of Supremacy as then framed was one that no Catholic elected to the House of Commons could possibly consent to take. The King was not moved by the argument, probably he did not listen to much of it, very likely was thinking of something else for most of the time, and he could only go back to his former declaration, that he would not allow the slightest alteration in the Oath of Supremacy, and would, therefore, refuse his consent to the whole scheme which the memorandum had set forth. The Ministers took the announcement with composure but firmly maintained their advice. Then the King blandly asked them what course they proposed to take; the three Ministers answered that they proposed to ask his Majesty for permission to announce to the House of Lords and to the House of Commons that they had ceased to hold office, and were no longer responsible for the policy of the country. George did not seem to have expected quite so prompt and decisive a reply; but he retained his outward composure—it must be remembered that he was in his own estimation and by his own professions the first gentleman in Europe—and he graciously said that he supposed he had no right to blame them for the course they felt bound to take.

He carried his graciousness still further, for, in the words of one of the Ministers, "the King took leave of us with great composure and great kindness, gave to each of us a salute on each cheek, and accepted our resignation of office." Satire itself could hardly burlesque that scene. Thackeray has made delicious fun of it in one of his lectures. Fancy the worn-out old Royal rake pressing a kiss on each cheek of the Duke and the Lord Chancellor and Sir Robert Peel and dismissing them as it were with his paternal blessing!

As soon as the dismissed Ministers had gone the King found that the difficulties of the crisis had only begun for him. It was absolutely impossible for him to get any responsible statesman to form a Ministry. He was at all events relieved of all trouble so far as Lord Grey was concerned, for even if he could so far have controlled his personal feelings as to overcome his dislike to Lord Grey, it would be utterly out of the question to think of inviting Lord Grey to form a Government which was not to admit the claims of the Catholics. Even George IV., with all his self-conceit and all his lack of sense, could not think of facing the country with the announcement that he had no longer any Ministers, and that he proposed to govern the country by despotic right. Even George knew that things had not yet come to such a pass with the people of England that they would stand an announcement of that kind. There was nothing for it but to give in, and the King gave in. He wrote to the Duke of Wellington telling him of his submission, and asking the Duke to urge Peel

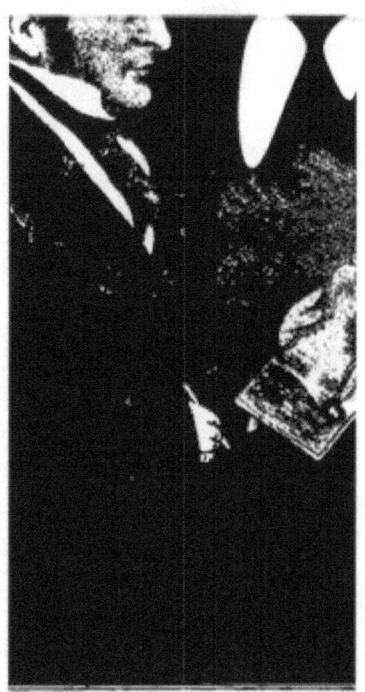

MALLORD WILLIAM TURNER, R.A.
(1775–1851.)

and Peel's colleagues to remain in office and bring in their scheme of Irish policy. The Constitution had conquered and the Sovereign was down. Peel brought in his measure of Catholic Emancipation and it was carried through both Houses of Parliament without much of a struggle. The Clare election had in fact proved a peaceful revolution. It has to be added that the measure when carried into law proved to be stinting and ungenerous in its concessions. It was constructed, to a large extent, on that principle of "checks and balances" about which so much was heard at a later period of English political life. The "checks and balances" idea was to take away a good deal with one hand, while giving something considerable with the other. The Bill abolished some old existing franchises in Ireland which, in the coming condition of things, might have proved too favourable to the Irish Catholics. The object to be gained was no doubt to put difficulties in the way of any triumph for the Catholics like that of the Clare election at any future day. Peel, we may be sure, would have made the measure more simple and complete if he had had his way; but he had to take into consideration the Tories and the House of Lords, and he did not think it wise to venture upon anything which might seem like an absolute surrender, even to the claims of justice, when those claims were put forward by Irish Roman Catholics. O'Connell in especial was ungenerously dealt with. After the passing of the Act he had to go back to Clare and to be elected all over again, just as if his previous elections had not been the moving occasion of the whole political crisis. Of course O'Connell had no trouble in getting re-elected; but there was something lamentable in the policy which only allowed him to come into Parliament when it was no longer humanly possible to keep him out. O'Connell took his seat in the House of Commons unchallenged, and with his entrance into Parliament a new chapter in history opened.

VIII

COMING REFORM CASTS ITS SHADOW BEFORE

THE first impulse to the Reform cause in England was undoubtedly given by the great French Revolution. Another impulse in the same way was given during the closing years of George IV. by a much smaller, swifter, and less blood-stained revolution—the revolution which overthrew Charles X., the last legitimist Sovereign of France—that modern times have seen or are likely to see. Charles X. succeeded Louis XVIII., who had been reseated on the French throne by the armies of England, Austria, Prussia, and Russia, and who represented the elder branch of the Bourbon family. It was well said—the words indeed have passed into a proverb—that the Bourbons learnt nothing and forgot nothing. Charles X. had learnt nothing from all the evidences of the growth of popular sentiment, and forgotten nothing of the ancestral claims of the Bourbons. He and his Ministers, among whom the most influential was the Prince de Polignac, found themselves confronted by a great crisis in France, and they set to work to deal with it after the characteristic Bourbonian fashion. De Polignac was a man of great ability, of inexorable stubbornness, into whose mind it was impossible for any ray of a new political idea to enter. The King and he alike took alarm at the freedom, to them intolerable, which the newspapers of France and especially of Paris began to exhibit in their criticisms of Ministers and of ministerial policy. There was nothing in the writings of the French Press which could seem surprising to an experienced English statesman, or which indeed such a statesman would not have taken for granted. But to Polignac and Polignac's master it seemed unbearable that the newspaper writers should arrogate to themselves the right of objecting to the policy of Ministers, the right of ridiculing it and denouncing it and holding it up to public scorn and anger.

The King and his Ministers had for a while contrived to get the assent of the two chambers—the Senate and the House of Representatives—to sanction their narrow and reactionary policy. But it might have been plain to any intelligent mind that the feeling of the country was rising against the conduct of the majority in both Houses, and that a General Election would send a very different majority into the Representative Chamber. The French people were then, as they are now, a newspaper-reading people; every journal published in Paris was eagerly read except, indeed, the one or two official papers which merely registered the views of the King and his Ministers and admonished the people to be taught by them. The people as a whole responded to the admonition by declining to read the Ministerial journals. There was a further cause of hostile feeling to the King's Ministers found in the fact that they were supposed to be in secret alliance with the King of England and his great Minister, the Duke of Wellington. The very name of Wellington was at that time a sound of horror in the ears of the French public. It was much too soon to forget that he had been the leading instrument in the policy which crushed the great Revolution, so far as that revolution was represented by Napoleon, and put back the heir of the Bourbons on the throne of France. Now there is not the least reason to suppose that the Duke of Wellington encouraged, or would have encouraged, the King of France and his admirers in the repressive measures which they intended to adopt. The Duke of Wellington as an English statesman had always shown himself obstinate enough in opposing every reform, but he proved through his whole career in office that he knew when a popular movement could no longer be resisted without bloodshed, and that he knew, in fact, when to give way. But the French public only saw in him the man who had compelled France to take back her Bourbon sovereigns, and his supposed friendship with Polignac was a new crime of Polignac's in the eyes of the great majority of Frenchmen.

The King and his Ministers at last made up their minds to coerce the French Press into silence. The Government issued a series of Ordinances which, if they could have been carried out, would have actually extinguished the liberty of the Press in

France. One of the Ordinances was that no newspaper should be offered for sale, or be allowed in any portion to leave the place in which it was printed, until five complete days had elapsed from the period of its preparation, and during the five days each journal was to be submitted to a Government censorship, and was not to be offered to the public until every omission and alteration had been made which the censor thought necessary to the dignity of the Crown. The penalties for disobedience were to be found in heavy fines and in confiscation of the whole edition. A heavy fine was ordained for any comment on the private life of any living Frenchman without the express permission of the person to whom the criticism referred, and if that particular person happened to be too indifferent or too magnanimous to make any quarrel about the matter, it was provided that the Public Prosecutor should take up the case whether the aggrieved person liked it or not. The most intense excitement broke out all over France. The purpose of the new policy was at once understood everywhere. The Courts of Law, which had judges faithful to the honourable traditions of the Bench, declined to pass sentences on journalists who had refused to regard the Ordinances of the King, and declared that the Ordinances themselves were a breach of the Constitution. The King lost his head under these conditions, and showed his temper on more than one occasion to the judges who had preferred the Constitution and the Law to the favour of the Sovereign. When the King appeared in public he was received in absolute silence. There

JOHN CONSTABLE, R.A.
(1776–1837.)

was a certain amount of rioting here and there in Paris and in the provinces, but nothing to alarm a stubborn Minister; and the King firmly believed that like Macbeth he could make his will avouch any course of action he thought fit to adopt. But even the King must have been profoundly impressed by the conspiracy of silence which seemed to surround him whenever he made his appearance in public. Furthermore, there were close observers in the higher ranks of the army itself who began to be more and more convinced from day to day that the troops could not be relied upon to act against the citizens of Paris.

The King still complacently hoped for the best, according to his interpretation of the word. There had been an expedition to Algiers in consequence of a quarrel between the French Government and the Dey of Algiers, and the latest military exploit of the Bourbons had been the conquest of the territory which we now know as Algeria. The King was possessed by the hope that the glory of this conquest would be enough to turn away public contention from any minor questions at home such as that of liberty of the Press, and the right of public speech; but the conquest of Algiers was not quite like one of Napoleon's victories, and the public of France kept on clamouring for reform without seeming to concern themselves about the new annexation of territory. Then again, to make matters worse for the King, there had been a bad winter and spring, the supplies of food were stinted, and the mere throwing out of employment of the vast number of workers who depended on the printing offices for their wages, was of itself enough to strengthen and embitter the popular discontent. The troops themselves were but ill provided for, and soldiers called out for special duty were sometimes left with hardly anything to eat or drink. Yet the King and his Ministers went their way as if the road lay smooth before them. There were prosecutions after prosecutions, which only made matters worse, and the King had now the majority of the Representative Chamber against him. He endeavoured to strengthen himself in the Senate by creating a large number of new Peers; but the struggle had gone too far to be seriously affected by any such measure, and the new Peers had little inclination to set themselves against the whole public of France. The King had now the best of the judges against him—it is to the honour of the Bench of Justice in almost every country that it has so often stood out against the despotic decrees of a Sovereign who chose to set aside the Constitution. The King went on from bad to worse; he dissolved the Chamber of Deputies on the ground that during the recent elections means had been used in various parts of the country to deceive the electors and prevail on them to disregard the wishes of the Sovereign. He went so far as even to set aside the provisions of the charter itself, to reduce the number of deputies in the Representative Chamber, and to alter their qualification and the methods by which they were elected. Sometimes, indeed, he seemed to waver in his purpose, and to be willing to come to terms with the people; but whenever he did thus waver he wavered at the wrong time, and found that it was too late, and then fell back on his rigid original determination. The officer in command of the troops at that time was Marshal Marmont, one of Napoleon's old generals, who had taken service under the King after Napoleon's fall, and had done his duty loyally, but who had little heart for the sort of work that now seemed to be set before him. In Paris the Republican Tricolor was flying everywhere, the people had begun to erect barricades in the streets—Miss Martineau, in her "History of the Peace," says that in relation to these events there first appeared in the London *Annual Register* the words, then new in such sense to the British public, "barricade" and "omnibus." Marshal Marmont sent to St. Cloud, where the King was staying, an aide-de-camp with a letter describing all that was going on in the capital. The messenger delivered the letter to the King himself, urging that an instant reply should be given; and then followed a memorable question and answer, "Is it a revolt? asked the King. "No, sire," was the answer, "it is not a revolt—it is a revolution." Then the King in despair offered to abdicate the Crown in favour of his grandson, the child of the Duke de Berri, who, he believed, would have a better chance than the King's own son. But the time had gone too far for any such arrangement as that. There had been fighting in the streets of Paris, and the fact that the revolution was not more deeply soaked in blood—the numbers killed on both sides being somewhere about a thousand, and the wounded in proportion—was due only to the conduct of most of the troops, who positively refused to fire on the people, or to take any part in the suppression of the popular movement. In fact, the revolution was accomplished. The King and his family escaped and found a refuge in England. Prince Polignac and others of the Ministry were tried and sentenced to life-long terms of imprisonment, but released by amnesty in 1836. The son of Philippe Egalité was proclaimed King, not of France, but of the French; and mounted the throne as King Louis Philippe, whom Carlyle afterwards described as "struggling under sad circumstances, to be called King of the French for a season," and it should be added in justice to Carlyle's power of prophetic vision that he used the words long before Louis Philippe's reign seemed likely to come to an abrupt end. Louis Philippe was set up as King of the Barricades, and Charles X. had by this time found a refuge in Holyrood Palace, Edinburgh, where he had been sheltered during his former exile from France. There was the end of the elder branch of the Bourbons.

Before this end had quite arrived the career of George IV. had come to a close. George had been sinking in health for some time, and at last it became evident to all observers that his life could not long endure. His latest acts as a Sovereign had been in keeping with the policy of his reign and of his Regency. He set his face rigidly against all reforms, and, indeed, unconsciously did what he could to make his death seem a relief to the great majority of his people. The rising generation could remember nothing of the hopes with which he had once inspired the public mind. They knew of him only as a man cursed with indolence and dandyism and dissipation. The nation had grieved, indeed, when his only daughter died, because it was felt everywhere that, should she succeed to the crown, the Empire would be blessed with the rule of an enlightened, a virtuous, and a noble-hearted sovereign. But the fates ruled it otherwise; and perhaps in losing his daughter, George lost the only human being whom he really loved, and who would have loved him if she could, if his selfishness, his worthlessness, and his occasional bursts of harshness would have allowed her. George IV. was succeeded by his brother, William IV., Duke of Clarence, who had been trained for the sea, and had proved a most unmanageable and unruly officer. William IV. was accepted as king with composure by most of his subjects, and with a certain renewed hopefulness by few on both sides. There were those on the Tory side who still thought it not impossible that the new king might be able to hold his own against the rising movement in favour of Constitutional Reform. There were a few on the Liberal side who thought that William IV., coming to royal power for the first time at an advanced age, would have acquired experience enough to teach him that the day had gone by when a king could make himself an effective barrier against the movement of the times. The English public, on the whole, even including the most advanced reformers, were well inclined to give the new king a fair chance. Some of the reformers, indeed, were comforted by the conviction that their movement had now gone too far to be long delayed by any influence. All sorts of stories had long been in circulation about William IV., about his unmanageable character as a naval officer, about his fluctuations in opinion, his love affairs, and his occasional eccentricity of conduct; but the more philosophical observers consoled themselves with the thought that he was probably less obstinate than George III., and was certainly less immoral than George IV. He had, at all events, one great recommendation to the bulk of his subjects, and that was found in the fact that he was the Sailor King. Therefore, it is only fair to say that the new king started with every prospect of a reasonable chance to succeed in the work of government. But the impulse towards reform had been immensely accelerated by the Three Days of July, as they were called, the three days which made a second revolution in France. When the news of that revolution was brought to Sir Robert Peel, who was then sitting in the House of Commons, his comment on it was that that was just what must come of an attempt to govern on too narrow a constitutional basis. The English people saw this distinctly; they saw that Paris had gone into revolt because Charles X. endeavoured to govern the country by himself, and by his Ministers, without any regard for the sentiments and the wishes of the vast majority of his people. They knew that he had endeavoured to maintain his rule by the suppression of political criticism and the freedom of speech; they knew, too, that one of his offences in the eyes of the French people had been his supposed deference to

the views of George IV. and the Duke of Wellington. The English people looked at home, and they saw that in their country also the King had been endeavouring to govern by his own will, and through the action of his favourite Ministers, and they had learned by the proceedings in many courts of law that the dearest wish of the Sovereign was to prevent all freedom of political criticism, whether in speech or in writing, and that the English King, like the French King, was striving to maintain his policy without the slightest regard for the wishes, the feelings, the aspirations and the convictions of the vast majority of the people. It would be impossible that the patriotic intelligence of England should not learn a lesson from the overthrow of Charles X. There was no desire whatever outside the ranks of a few very extreme thinkers and declaimers for the establishment of a republican system in these countries. Many years later a great English orator said that among the population of these countries the question of a republic had not come up. It certainly had not come up, had not even dawned at the time when William IV. ascended the throne; but there was at least a hope that the new king might do better than either George III. or George IV. had done; and a confident belief that in any case the Reform movement could not be long delayed. Therefore the change from one Sovereign to another passed off quietly, and people in general awaited the coming of new events without unreasonable expectation, but also without marked distrust, and certainly without any dismay.

The new Kings of England and France seemed alike disposed to seek for popularity among the humbler of their subjects. William IV. walked about the London streets with his umbrella tucked under his arm and talked familiarly with every one he knew, and even when on great State occasions he had to wear his Royal robes, he wore his naval uniform under them. Louis Philippe too walked about the streets of Paris just as he thought fit, became identified with his umbrella, and was known throughout his reign as the "Bourgeois King." Lord Eldon took alarm at what he considered King William's over-familiarity with people in general, and laid it down as an axiom that a king, in order to maintain his throne, must show in his ordinary demeanour that he considered himself the superior of everybody else in the world. When William came to the throne he found the Duke of Wellington in office as Prime Minister, with Sir Robert Peel as Home Secretary, and he announced in the most off-hand and informal way that he had no ill-feeling whatever towards his good friend the Duke of Wellington, in whom, and in Sir Robert Peel, he placed the highest confidence. The existing Parliament would, of course, have to be dissolved. It was the rule then, and continued to be so down to a comparatively recent period, that a dissolution of Parliament must follow the death of a sovereign. The King sent a formal message to Parliament almost immediately after his accession, in which he dwelt, according to the usual ceremonial fashion, on the loss the nation had sustained by the death of the late Sovereign, and then went on to say that the sooner the new elections took place the better. This was not exactly what the public had expected. The King was at this time sixty-five years of age, and was not in particularly robust health; and the heir to the throne was the Princess Victoria, a child then only eleven years old. People asked themselves what was to happen in the meantime, supposing the King were to die suddenly, were to meet with some fatal accident, since no one had been appointed Regent, to carry on the Government until the young princess should come to the age when, according to constitutional law, it would be possible for her to perform the duties of a queen.

Parliament has to give its consent to the nomination of a Regent, and everybody naturally expected that the King would make some intimation to both Houses on the subject. Nothing about the Regency was said in the King's message, and the public disappointment was very widespread and deeply felt. There were gloomy forebodings in many a mind. One grim and darksome figure stood in the shadow of the throne, the figure of the Duke of Cumberland, the King's eldest surviving brother. It would be hard now to bring home to the ordinary reader any adequate idea of the hatred which was felt by the mass of the English people for the Duke of Cumberland. If that prince were guilty of half the offences laid to his charge, he would have been better suited for a contemporary of the days of Caligula, or of Cæsar Borgia, than for a member of the royal family of England in 1830. Moreover, the Duke of Cumberland would at once become, in the event of the King's death, the successor to the crown of Hanover. The Georges were all Kings of Great Britain and of Hanover, and the Hanoverian crown descended in the male line only. What might not happen, it was asked, if the guardianship of the young princess were suddenly to be left, in the event of the King's death, to the care of her eldest uncle, the Duke of Cumberland? Men believed the Duke of Cumberland capable of anything. We shall see later on how there spread through England a strong conviction that the Duke of Cumberland was putting himself at the head of an organised conspiracy to alter the succession, and assume the crown himself. This fear had not, at that time, taken a shape so definite, even in the minds of alarmists, as it afterwards came to bear. But even then popular opinion was ready to believe in the possibility of any dark deed being sanctioned by the Duke of Cumberland. Even those who were not alarmists, and were not disposed to exaggerate the demerits of the Duke of Cumberland, kept asking what was to happen if on the King's death he were to betake himself to his kingdom of Hanover, and try to organise conspiracies there. Every one knows how hated in England became the very name of Hanover during the reigns of George I. and II.; how the people believed that every English interest was sacrificed by the Sovereign's love for his Hanoverian crown, and how jealous and impatient public opinion had become in these countries. There were, indeed, not a few who would have been well contented if the Duke of Cumberland, on succeeding to the Hanoverian throne, were to go to Hanover and stay there, and never bestow a thought upon England any more. This, however, was exactly what most people believed that the Duke of Cumberland would never do. The common belief was that he would make of Hanover a convenient retreat for the organisation of conspiracy against the child-sovereign of England. People looked forward, therefore, with gloomy forebodings to the dangers that might be threatened if the King were to die, and the Duke of Cumberland, no Regent being named, were to succeed at once to the Crown of Hanover and the guardianship of the Princess Victoria. The first disappointment which King William gave to his people was by the omission in his Royal message of any allusion to the appointment of a Regent.

On the 30th of July, Lord Grey in the House of Lords, and Lord Althorp in the House of Commons, moved for the delay of a day in replying to the Royal message. The motive of the delay was perfectly well understood; it was simply in order to give time for the consideration of the course which ought to be taken with regard to the Royal message if the King should not in the meantime make any suggestion as to the appointment of a Regent. The Duke of Wellington, on behalf of the Government, refused to agree to any proposal for delay, and although several Tory Peers, including the indomitable Lord Eldon himself, voted in favour of Lord Grey's motion, the Ministers carried with them a majority of forty-four in the House of Lords, and of forty-six in the House of Commons. The debate in the House of Commons deserves notice, if only for the passion which Henry Brougham threw into it, and the extraordinary demeanour of the House itself. Brougham, of course, supported the Liberal policy in the House of Commons, and his language was certainly well calculated to provoke a scene in an excitable assembly. Somebody interrupted Brougham with a peculiar cry which was undoubtedly meant for an imitation of the utterance of one of the lower animals, on which Brougham observed that by a wonderful disposition of Nature every animal had its peculiar mode of expressing itself, and he was too much of a philosopher to quarrel with any of those modes. Under the circumstances, Brougham may be said to have dealt good-humouredly enough with the interruption. O'Connell, at a day a little later, met with some peculiarly clamorous interruptions from a great number of voices, whereupon, in tones of thunder, he called upon the owners of the voices to "silence their beastly bellowing." The Speaker ruled that O'Connell was out of order in using the word "beastly," whereupon O'Connell blandly declared that in deference to the Speaker he withdrew the adjective, but he added, "I never heard or read of any bellowing which was not beastly." Brougham's speech on the occasion to which we are particularly referring was met by many such interruptions, and in that debate, as in most debates in the House of Commons, when passion is at all aroused, men indulged themselves in any form of interruption which suited their tastes or their lungs. One Honourable Member, perhaps, had the gift of imitating the bellowing of a bull; another preferred to bleat like a sheep; a third reproduced with full artistic effect the noise of a crowing cock ; a fourth mewed like a cat ; and so on, with imitations of the whole animal kingdom, among which even the mellifluous, and probably in certain instances most appropriate, voice of the donkey sounded in the ears of those who cared to listen. Some of the descriptions given to us by men who were present during certain of these noisy scenes, would seem hardly credible to many who even now think the House of Commons a rather uproarious and disorderly assembly. All this, it should be observed, took place at a time when Parliament was still unreformed, when the vulgar herd had no power to vote for the election of a member of the House of Commons, and when one of the great arguments against Reform was that it would flood that House with uneducated and noisy persons. Brougham certainly, sometimes, gave an excuse for angry interruptions. In the course of his speech, to which we have been referring, he made a vehement attack on Sir Robert Peel and the other Ministers present. He had been complaining of the policy of the Duke of Wellington, and he suddenly said, looking fixedly at Peel : " Him I accuse not. It is you I accuse—his flatterers—his mean, fawning parasites." The House of Commons in our day is noisy enough sometimes, and rude enough in its personal attacks, but such words as these would be impossible there now.

England lost about this time a remarkable man on a most remarkable occasion. The death of such a man must always have a deep personal and historical interest; but the occasion which indirectly led to that death was an event of the highest importance to England and to civilisation. It was the opening of the first railway of any length completed in this country. There was a great ceremonial on the 15th of September, 1830, in honour of the opening of the line from Liverpool to Manchester. The Duke of Wellington, Sir Robert Peel, and many other men took part in the ceremony, which was to have been followed by a great public dinner at Manchester. Mr. Huskisson was one of those who attended. He had been paying a visit to his constituents in Liverpool, and, although in very feeble health, he had made up his mind to be present on the memorable occasion of the opening of this first completed railway. Before the train left Liverpool the railway authorities requested the company to keep their places in the carriages until the train reached its destination, and a printed handbill, setting forth the request, was passed along among the travellers. It seems almost unnecessary to say that the request and caution were of no avail. The train stopped at a wayside station a few miles down the line, and several of the company immediately got out and indulged their curiosity by walking up and down and inspecting the outside of the carriages. Unluckily, a friend of the Duke of Wellington and of Huskisson was seized with the idea that this would be a propitious moment to bring the two men together and get them to shake hands. The idea spread abroad, and both the Duke and Huskisson were quite willing to take this opportunity of renewing their former friendship. The Duke advanced along the platform to meet Mr. Huskisson, who was approaching him, and held out his hand in cordial greeting. Before Huskisson had well time to take the proffered hand some alarm was caused by the reported approach of a locomotive, and a cry was raised to those who were standing outside admonishing them to get into the carriages again. Huskisson was standing by the open door of one of the carriages, and was not quick in getting in, probably because of his physical weakness. The open door at which he stood was struck by the locomotive, and Huskisson received injuries so severe that he died almost immediately after being removed to a neighbouring parsonage. The fatal event, of course, cast the deepest gloom over the whole party; the Ministers were only induced not to break up the ceremonial at once by the fear that some terrible alarm might be spread over Manchester. This was again a season of alarms, and no one could tell what exaggerated form bewildered rumour might not take if none of the members were to arrive at the place of their destination. Nothing seemed more probable than that an affrighted tale might be spread about the assassination of the Ministers of the Crown in a body, and might lead to the widest disturbances. In any case it was earnestly urged upon the Ministers that the death of Mr. Huskisson might be set down as one of the inevitable consequences of venturing on a railway journey, and that the prospects of the whole railway system might be severely damaged for some time to come. The Ministers, therefore, went to Manchester, but the public celebration of the event was put off. In Huskisson England lost one who might almost be called a great statesman. The stranger who visits Liverpool to-day will find Huskisson's name maintained in streets and squares, and docks and public institutions.

We have said that this particular time was a season of alarm once again. There was great distress and, of course, consequent discontent throughout many parts of the country. The fierce passion for destruction which had formerly broken out in and around the towns, and had led to the breaking of machinery, now showed itself in the country places, and in the destruction of corn-ricks and farmhouses. One of the favourite arguments of Tories and Reactionaries when the Revolution of 1830 broke out in France was founded on the actions of some of the agricultural populations of that country. A sudden mania had set in there for the destruction of farmhouses and stores of corn. "What could you do with such a people," it was indignantly asked, "but to keep them down by force, to shoot them down, to crush them by any and every means? What was the wrong-doing of Charles X. but that he had been too slow to use the weapons in his possession for the wholesale putting down of such acts of crime?" And now, behold, the very same phenomenon was visible in many parts of England. The passion spread from county to county. The cant name of "Swing" was used as typical of the rick-burning outlaw; and swing indeed a great many men did for their share or their supposed share in the business. At that time there was no idea of putting down violence but by greater violence. The gallows was in full use almost everywhere, and even boys were remorselessly hanged for their share or their supposed share in the doings of "Swing." No one, of course, could possibly justify or excuse this rage for wanton destruction. Such a rage, however, is a common outcome of popular and social discontent, and when it does break out it ought to be regarded as a subject to be discussed as well as a crime to be punished. As usually happens in such cases, an impression got abroad that many of the acts of destruction were prepared and instigated by paid emissaries of the authorities, who were glad to commend themselves to their masters by promoting outrages which might tend to cast discredit upon all popular movements in favour of reform. The Funds went down, and alarmists began to predict that if the Government did not show a firm front the revolution in France would be followed by a revolution in England. Even in the minds of many who did not carry their feelings of alarm quite so far as this, an impression began to prevail that a serious crisis was again approaching, that the Sailor King or Patriot King was already losing his popularity, and that a great division was again taking place between the Sovereign and his people. Some even of the strongest Tories began to think that the Duke of Wellington would have to go out of office before long. According to their ideas he had not been explicit enough and decided enough in his condemnation of the Reform movement, and the disturbed state of the country was mainly owing to his lack of firmness in dealing with the whole crisis.

In the meantime the new Parliament met, and the King's speech was made public. The speech disappointed all popular expectation. The King recommended, indeed, that steps should be taken to provide for a Regency in case of his death, but otherwise there was nothing said which could tend to conciliate the people. The Royal speech expressed the determination of the King to maintain all the treaties by which the political systems of the Continent had been forcibly reconstructed, condemned with stern emphasis and frequent repetition the disturbances in Great Britain and Ireland, pledged all the powers of the State to put down and properly punish such disturbances, and, indirectly at least, associated these disturbances with the popular movement in favour of Constitutional Reform by an inflated passage about the inestimable blessings of living amid such political institutions as those which then existed in these countries. In the midst of all the prevailing commotion Mr. Brougham gave notice in the House of Commons that it was his intention to bring forward on a day which he named—a day then only a fortnight off—the whole question of Parliamentary Reform. Brougham was then probably the most popular man in England, the recognised leader of the Reform movement.

IX

THE GREAT REFORM BILL

A NEW Parliament met on October 26, 1830. The opening debate was as usual on the Address in reply to the Speech from the Throne, and it proved to be a debate of the greatest importance. The Government were challenged by Lord Grey and others to make known their views on the subject of Parliamentary Reform; and the Government, through the mouth of the Prime Minister, the Duke of Wellington, did make known their views with a vengeance. All that the Duke of Wellington could accord to any proposal for Parliamentary Reform was, if we may adopt certain famous words then still ringing in the ears of Europe, "La mort sans phrase." The Duke declared himself utterly opposed to any and every measure which called for an alteration in the existing parliamentary system. He declared that he had never read or even heard of any scheme which satisfied his mind that the parliamentary system could be rendered any better than it was at the moment. The country, he declared, was happy enough to possess a legislature which answered all the good purposes of legislation, and that to a degree never before known in any other country. The whole system of representation and of voting possessed, he insisted, the absolute confidence of the public. He flung into the face of Lord Grey the announcement that he did not intend to propose any scheme which involved any alteration of the constitution. But he was not even content with that proclamation; he went a little further and announced that so long as he held a position in any Government he should always feel it his duty to resist any such proposal when brought forward by others.

The delivery of such a speech clearly settled the question as to the Duke's possessing any faculty of statesmanship, supposing such a question possible. Almost anybody else in such a position as this would have thought it enough to say that he himself did not believe the existing constitution could be improved upon, and that he therefore did not propose to bring forward any measure for its improvement. But it would not be like the Duke to content himself with such a reply. He felt himself bound to go much further, and to declare that it was absolutely beyond the wit of man to devise or suggest any possible improvement, and that therefore he should feel it his bounden duty to oppose any proposition brought forward by no matter whom, which began with the daring and impious suggestion that there could be any room for improvement in the constitution which the wisdom of our ancestors had bequeathed to us. The Duke's speech certainly did not sound the death-knell of Reform; but it did sound the death-knell of the Wellington Administration. The country had quite outgrown the time when it could take the doctrine from any one, that no improvement could ever again be made in our best of all possible constitutions. The Duke's colleagues saw already that the end of their time had come.

The country blazed into a fury of passion when the words of the Duke of Wellington were known; and the Ministry became more unpopular probably than even a Tory Ministry ever was before or since in England. On the other hand, the popularity of the King went up at this crisis. There was a general idea abroad that William was not likely to encourage or stand by such declarations as that of the Duke of Wellington. He had been popular at one time, chiefly by contrast with the more recent policy of his predecessor, and there was a general hope that the Patriot King, as he was called, would turn back to the path of his former popularity. It is not, perhaps, quite easy to understand just now why such high expectations were formed of William IV.; but at all events, those who believed that he would not press his general likings and dislikings to the verge of revolution had reason afterwards to congratulate themselves on their optimism. The question with most of the Ministers was now not how to keep in office, but how to get decently out of office. Every one, with perhaps the single exception of the Duke of Wellington, must have seen that the public feeling against the Tory Government was too strong to be long resisted; and the Duke of Wellington, to do him justice, did not care whether he was in office or out of office so long as he believed that he had done what he considered his duty. The end came about by what might almost be called a matter of accident. Sir Henry Parnell brought forward a motion in the House of Commons asking for the appointment of a Select Committee to take into consideration the estimates and amounts proposed by his Majesty regarding the Civil List. Sir Henry Parnell, who afterwards became Lord Congleton, was one of the family of the poet who was popular in the days of Swift and Addison, and was an ancestor of the Charles Stewart Parnell whose name was afterwards famous in the debates of the House of Commons. Sir Henry Parnell's motion was carried by a majority of twenty-nine, although the Government had thrown all the strength they had into opposing it. The motion was in itself hardly one of first-class importance. A Ministry anxious to cling to office might easily have taken the sting out of it by promising some sort of concession, or might have allowed it to pass without any further notice, as is done with so many a resolution brought forward by a private member, and not directly concerning any Ministerial scheme actually before the House. But the circumstances were peculiar, and the Government thought it best to accept the passing of the resolution as a vote of censure; they took advantage of the opportunity, fearing that if they were to hold to office they might be defeated a little later on some subject more serious and critical in the eyes of the country. It is quite possible, too, that they may have thought it a good stroke of policy to accept defeat in a controversy which left to them the appearance of having forfeited office while defending the prerogative of the Sovereign against Whigs, Radicals, and Revolutionists. Whatever the deciding reason their course was promptly taken. Next morning they tendered their resignation to the King, and the resignation was promptly accepted. Later that same day the House of Commons was informed that the Duke of Wellington's Administration had ceased to exist, and the conviction was borne in upon every mind, that Lord Grey, with his Reform scheme, must become the head of the next Government. The anticipation was, of course, fulfilled; Lord Grey was at once sent for by the King and invited to form an administration.

The main interest as to the members of the new administration attached to Henry Brougham and to Lord John Russell, the Earl Russell of a later day. Brougham was to be Lord Chancellor, and the news of his appointment created a wild display of anger among his opponents. Brougham had made many enemies; in his outbursts of overwhelming and reckless eloquence he had spared no opposing force, man or institution, that came in his way. In the House of Commons he had sometimes denounced his antagonists with epithets such as no Speaker would now allow to be uttered in that assembly. The position of Lord Chancellor is one of the very gravest and the most dignified that a British subject can be called upon to occupy. It is not, indeed, a position of great political influence, for the Lord Chancellor is not expected to take frequent part in the debates of the House of Lords; and, of course, it is assumed that he will not there display himself as a political partisan. Nor is he in actual fact what he is very often called, the Speaker of the House of Lords, for he has nothing like the control over the Lords which every Speaker has over the House of Commons. If a number of members rise together the Speaker calls on one of them, and in the ordinary course of life his decision is accepted without dispute. But if a number of Peers rise together, each claiming to be heard, the Lord Chancellor has no power to decide who is to address the assembly. The Lords decide that for themselves by a vote of their own, if necessary. Nor has the Lord Chancellor any right, such as the Speaker of the House of Commons has, to decide upon all points of order; that right, too, the Peers retain for themselves. Still the position of Lord Chancellor is very high and is very dignified. The Lord Chancellor is declared to be the keeper of the Sovereign's conscience, and all the Tories were furious with anger at the thought of Henry Brougham being exalted to such a place. The King, indeed, himself objected to Brougham's being made Lord Chancellor; but he was prevailed upon by Lord Grey to withdraw his opposition and consent to the appointment. Lord Grey, at one moment of the controversy, suggested a possible compromise. He advised that Brougham should be made Master of the Rolls—a position next in rank to that of Lord Chancellor; but that as a sop to Brougham's well-known love of political debate, he should be allowed to retain his seat in the House of Commons.

King William made to this the very shrewd and sensible objection, that to make Brougham Master of the Rolls, and allow him still to sit in the House of Commons, would be to give him very high office and full freedom of debate as well; and the King added that there was no knowing whom Brougham might not attack if he were allowed the chance. Lord Grey pointed out that it would be utterly impossible for any Ministry to carry any Reform Bill if the co-operation of Henry Brougham were not secured in some way. These may not seem very exalted considerations to govern a Prime Minister or a Sovereign in the Ministerial appointments, but Lord Grey knew well what a force he had to deal with when he was dealing with Brougham; and although he believed Brougham to be a thoroughly sincere reformer, yet he had to recognise the extraordinary degree of vanity that was in Brougham's nature, and it was clear to him that Brougham was not a man to be offended. Of course if Brougham had been left out of the Cabinet altogether he would not, and could not, have turned round and proclaimed himself hostile to the principle of political reform; but it would have been very easy for him while still retaining his character of advanced reformer, and even in sustenance of that very character, to keep on criticising every clause of the Bill, insisting that the Government did not go far enough here, and were proving false to past promises there, and thus appealing at the most convenient moments from half-hearted reformers in the House of Commons to whole-hearted reformers outside it. The Bill could in any case only be carried by the most judicious steersmanship and by the most extraordinary blending of courage and caution; and Lord Grey knew very well that with Brougham as an ungracious critic the measure could not be carried at all. Even as it was, some intimation seems to have got to Brougham that there was a delay over his appointment, and at first he seemed disposed to take offence and decline to hold any manner of office in the new administration. But Lord Grey contrived to get over Brougham's objections, as he had previously got over the objections raised by the King, and it was soon made known to the world that Henry Brougham, Harry Brougham as he was more usually called, was to be the new Lord Chancellor of England.

The other appointment in which great public interest was felt, although of a very different kind, was that of Lord John Russell, afterwards Earl Russell. Lord John Russell was regarded as a man of the most brilliant promise. He belonged to one of the great historic families of England, a family which had during successive centuries written its name in the English annals. As a boy, he had sat at the feet of Fox; and he was always a close friend of the Irish national poet, Thomas Moore. The writer of this book has often seen Moore's portrait in its place of honour in the house of the late Countess Russell, Lord John's widow. Russell had a genuine love for literature as well as for politics, and every literary man of his time was made welcome in his house. He had acted as private secretary to the Duke of Wellington during the Peninsular War, and had visited the great Napoleon at Elba, and had done his best to persuade Napoleon that there was not the slightest likelihood of Wellington attempting to seize the crown of England. Napoleon smiled and blandly submitted as to the judgment of an expert; but he did not seem absolutely convinced—what after all could be more natural than that a great military conqueror should cast a longing eye upon the crown of his master? Lord John Russell was a sincere and ardent champion of the claims of Catholic Emancipation, as he was indeed a champion of civil and religious liberty all over the world. He was a friend to Greece, and did all that came within his reach to forward the cause of Greek independence. His career, so far, in the House of Commons, had been full of promise. He never, perhaps, rose to the height of great parliamentary oratory; his presence was not commanding; and his voice, though clear and telling, was not strong or resonant. He was not a great orator as Robert Peel was, and as Gladstone and Bright afterwards were. But he was a perfect master of parliamentary fence; a most quick and dangerous antagonist. No one was happier with a bland incisive repartee, with an epigram which left something like a vitriolic burn behind it. Some of us can well remember Lord John Russell during his later years in the House of Commons and his years later still in the House of Lords. Some of us have often thought it deeply interesting to listen to Russell's words, if it were only for the reason that they were the words of a man who had talked with the great Napoleon at Elba.

But Russell's speeches never failed to be interesting in themselves; and they had the not common advantage of being as good to read as they were good to hear. The new Ministry has to be remembered for the fact, among other and greater facts, that Lord Palmerston entered into office under Whig auspices for the first time. Lord Palmerston became Foreign Secretary, and with that office all the best days of his parliamentary life were afterwards associated.

Lord Grey at once entrusted to Lord John Russell the principal conduct of the Reform Bill through the House of Commons; and Lord John Russell went into communication with Grey's son-in-law, Lord Durham, the Durham who, as John George Lambton, had rendered great public service to the Reform cause already, and who was to become celebrated afterwards as the man who composed the momentous strife between Canada and the mother country, and rendered Canada one of the most prosperous and loyal of all the British Colonies. Lord John Russell sketched a plan of Reform, which he submitted to Lord Durham. On the whole, Lord Durham approved of it with, however, certain amendments of his own, some of which Lord John Russell readily accepted. The plan was approved by Earl Grey, and was then submitted to the King himself, by whom it was, to adopt Lord John Russell's own words, readily and cheerfully sanctioned. But the scheme was kept a profound secret from the outer world. All Ministerial schemes are supposed to be profound secrets until the moment comes for expounding them in Parliament; but in the ordinary course of things the purport of most Ministerial schemes does happen to get known in political society somehow, and gives a subject of discussion to the clubs and the dinner tables for days and days before the authoritative exposition is made. In this case, however, the secret, although in the keeping of more than thirty men, was not allowed to get out to the public anywhere, and conjecture was busy as to what the new measure was to be even in the House of Commons itself on the very day when Lord John Russell was to make his statement. It was thought of the utmost importance by Grey and Russell and their colleagues that the opponents of Reform should not have an opportunity of tearing the Bill in pieces, or rather rending it by pieces, before the full Ministerial statement could be brought under the attention of the public. It must be remembered that in the House of Commons there were a good many anti-reformers not to be found on the benches of the Tory opposition. Many a professed Liberal, who, if once the public outside showed a determination to accept the Bill, would not have ventured to say a word against it, might yet have grasped at any chance of decrying certain of its details and turning attention away from its main purpose if he could have known beforehand what the precise contents of the measure were to be. Some particular clause, weak or positively defective in itself, some clause which in the course of the parliamentary proceedings could easily have been amended as the Bill passed through Committee, might have been made the means of creating a premature, irrelevant, and yet dangerous discussion, filling the mind of Reformers out of doors with the idea that the measure would never do.

On the 1st of March, 1831, Lord John Russell made his opening statement of the Government's proposals on the subject of Parliamentary Reform. Nothing could be more clear, more comprehensive, and in its way more eloquent than Russell's speech on that great occasion. The speech is even now a most interesting and a most important historical document. There is not, perhaps, anywhere to be found in our parliamentary records an exposition so complete and yet so concise of the reforms which it proposed to introduce and of the anomalies and the evils which it proposed to abolish. It seems hard now to understand how a State which at one time possessed a full understanding of the principle of a representative government and a system which very fairly corresponded with that principle should have come in the process of generations to lose all the reality of constitutional government, and to sink into a condition of things which was but the burlesque of a representative system. Russell's speech made it clear that this was the fact, and made it clear also how the fact had come to be in existence. "The ancient constitution of our country," said Lord John Russell in his opening sentences, "declares that no man should be taxed for the support of the State who has not consented by himself or by his representative to the imposition of those taxes." This, of course, is the keynote of the whole principle of representative government. It is not meant to be understood, as some of Russell's quibbling and feeble-minded opponents tried to make out in the course of the debate, that Lord John was laying down a principle which amounted to the absurdity that, if a man voted against a tax, he therefore ought not to be called upon to pay it. The meaning of Russell's words, which these right honourable and honourable members affected not to understand, could not have puzzled for one moment the mind even of a schoolboy far inferior in native understanding to the intelligent pupil who appears so often in Lord Macaulay's Essays. Russell's meaning was quite clear; and his exposition of the representative principle could not be disputed. The principle of representative government means that no man should be compelled to pay a tax who has not had an opportunity by himself or by his representative of expressing his opinion as to whether the tax was or was not one that ought to be imposed. Of course a majority must decide in the end, or there could be no representative government at all; for representative government is in its very essence government by majority. Lord John Russell showed that at one time this principle of representation did exist in England; and that it was provided by English law that each county should send to the House of Commons two Knights—a county member is still called in formal phrase a Knight of the Shire; each city, two burgesses; and each borough, two members. "Thus, no doubt," said Russell, "at that early period the House of Commons did represent the people of England. There is no doubt, likewise, that the House of Commons does not now represent the people of England." How the change came about has already been shown in these pages. The whole condition of the country had meanwhile been changing; some of the boroughs had dwindled away until they were left with no inhabitants at all, but the owner of the soil still continued to return himself as representative of the little desert to the House of Commons. Great towns and cities were springing up everywhere over the country, but these had come into existence too late to have the benefit of the old constitution; and the people of England had not yet exerted themselves to create a new constitution suited to the new times. There is one passage in Lord John Russell's speech which has indeed been often quoted already, but which cannot be quoted too often, cannot be read too often by students of English history, and should certainly not be omitted from this page. "A stranger who was told that this country is unparalleled in wealth and industry, and more civilised and more enlightened than any country was before it, that it is a country that prides itself on its freedom, and that once in every seven years it elects representatives from its population to act as the guardians and preservers of that freedom, would be anxious and curious to see how that representation is formed and how the people choose their representatives, to whose fate and guardianship they entrust their free and liberal constitution. Such a person would be very much astonished if he were taken to a ruined mound, and told that that mound sent two representatives to Parliament; if he were taken to a stone wall and told that three niches in it sent two representatives to

Parliament; if he were taken to a park where no houses were to be seen and told that that park sent two representatives to Parliament. But if he were told all this and were astonished at hearing it, he would be still more astonished if he were to see large and opulent towns, full of enterprise and industry and intelligence, containing vast magazines of every species of manufacture, and were then told that these towns sent no representatives to Parliament." Then Lord John went a step further, but in a different direction, for the purpose of giving his intelligent stranger a new chance of surprise. "Such a person," he said, "would be still more astonished if he were taken to Liverpool, where there is a large constituency, and told, here is a fine specimen of a popular election. He would see bribery employed to the greatest extent and in the most unblushing manner; he would see every voter receiving a number of guineas in a box as the price of his corruption; and after such a spectacle he would, no doubt, be much astonished that a nation whose representatives are thus chosen could perform the functions of legislation at all, and enjoy respect in any degree. The confidence of the country," Lord John went on to declare, "in the construction and constitution of the House of Commons is gone. It would be easier to transfer the flourishing manufactures of Leeds and Manchester to Gatton and Old Sarum than to re-establish confidence and sympathy between this House and those whom it calls its constituents."

Nothing could be more complete and correct as a picture than this vigorous outline which Lord John

Russell drew of the majestic fabric of the British constitution. Had he had time, or were it necessary to elaborate every detail, it is quite certain that the more he worked into the picture the more appalling would its fidelity become. The House of Commons listened with intense interest to this masterly exposition; and if votes were to be governed merely by philosophical conclusions or considerations of unselfish patriotism, there can be no doubt that the House must then and there have decided to accept the principle that reform of some kind was needed for such a constitution. But then came the question, What kind of reform had the Government to propose; and what sort of reform would the House of Commons be likely to accept? In judging of the merits of the whole measure, it is necessary to bear in mind that the House was divided on this subject into three classes of opinion. There was the opinion of those who in their hearts were opposed to all manner of reform; there was the opinion of those who would have liked what they considered a moderate and gradual change; and there was the opinion of those, strengthened by a great popular influence out of doors, who were not likely to be thoroughly satisfied with any measure which the Government might see their way to offer. It is not possible to appreciate the difficulty of Lord John Russell's task if we do not give due account to these considerations. Lord John Russell went on to explain that there were three principal grievances which the Government proposed to abolish. The first was the nomination of members by individual patrons; the second was the election of members by close corporations; and the third was the expense of elections, including the vast sums squandered on bribery and corruption. Now, to begin with, Lord John proposed to deprive all the really extinguished boroughs of any right of nomination whatever. The Gattons and Old Sarums, the green mounds and the park-walls, were no longer to be able at the command of the lord of the soil to send up a so-called representative to the House of Commons. Further, the Government proposed that no borough which had less than one thousand inhabitants should any longer be allowed to send a member to Parliament; and that no borough which had not more than four thousand inhabitants should be allowed to return more than one representative. By this process of reduction the number of members would become less than it was by one hundred and sixty-eight; and Lord John Russell explained that the Government did not mean to fill up the whole of these vacancies, believing, as they did, that the House of Commons had too many members already. Many years, more than a quarter of a century indeed, after this announcement John Bright complained that the House of Commons had still far too many members; and, as he put it in his blunt away, the House was sometimes an orderly and sometimes a disorderly mob, but that, orderly or disorderly, it was always a mob. Lord John Russell went on to say that the necessity for some reduction in the number of members in the House was all the more necessary, seeing that he hoped the attendance in future would be that of really working members; and that the Parliamentary

Roll would not contain the names of a great number of gentlemen who, when once they had obliged themselves or their patron by accepting an election to Parliament, took care to live their lives pleasantly abroad, and never troubled themselves to attend the debates and divisions in the House of Commons. Lord John Russell announced that it was intended to give two members each to seven large towns which had not had previously any manner of representation. It is something positively amusing now to read the names of the seven towns on which it was proposed to confer the right of representation for the first time. These towns were Manchester, Birmingham, Leeds, Greenwich, Wolverhampton, Sheffield, and Sunderland. Six at least of these towns may be said to represent—might even then be said to represent—the growing commercial prosperity and energy of England, as no other towns could possibly do. Twenty other towns of smaller size were to be represented each by one member. The metropolis itself was to have eight new members, two members each being given to the Tower Hamlets, Holborn, Finsbury, and Lambeth. Each of these metropolitan constituencies is now, and was even then, a big town in itself. The Government proposed to sweep away nearly all the complex franchises—the "fancy franchises," as they would have been called at a later day; franchises conferred in many instances by close corporations, often from selfish and corrupt motives, and some of which did not even carry with them as a qualification for the right to vote the condition that the voter must reside in the borough, whose representative he was privileged to join in electing. Lord John Russell proposed as far as possible to simplify the voting system, and to make it at least similar in principle for boroughs and for counties. In the boroughs a resident householder paying rates for a house of the yearly value of £10 and upwards was to be entitled to vote; in counties a copyholder to the value of £10 a year, who was also qualified to serve on juries, and a leaseholder for not less than twenty-one years, whose annual rent was not less than £50, were to become voters at once. Lord John Russell attempted to deal with the expenses of elections by an arrangement that the poll should be taken in separate districts, so that no voter should have to travel more than fifteen miles to record his vote; and also by limiting the duration of the poll to a period of not more than two days. It may be said at once that this part of the measure proved utterly inadequate to its purpose. Again and again have subsequent Governments been compelled to introduce new measures for the suppression and for the punishment of bribery. For more than forty years after the introduction of the first Reform Bill the question of bribery remained an open scandal, against which earnest reformers were never tired of declaiming. All that can be said of the Government of Earl Grey on this score is that they had an extraordinary piece of complicated work to undertake; and that to carry a really effective measure for the extinction of bribery at such a time would have been an utter impossibility. Hogarth's sketches of English electioneering days were hardly in the slightest degree caricatures of the system which prevailed in the time of the first Reform Bill, and indeed for many long years after its introduction. It is well worthy of notice, is indeed a very interesting fact, that in the speech which Russell made when moving for leave to bring in the Bill he spoke for the first time of his own friends and sympathisers as the Reform party, and he awarded to his opponents the title of Conservatives.

Lord John Russell, as has been said, merely moved for leave to bring in the Bill. That is one of the parliamentary forms of the House of Commons which is dispensed with in the House of Lords. Every Bill in both Houses must have three readings; but in the House of Lords the first reading is accorded as a matter of right to the member who introduces any measure. In the House of Commons, the first reading is represented by a motion that leave be given to bring in the Bill; and although that motion is not much opposed or much debated, still it can be discussed and can be opposed. The moment Lord John Russell had closed his speech, the Opposition flamed out at once. Sir Robert Harry Inglis was the first man to rise on the part of the Tory Opposition. Now Sir Robert Harry Inglis was a curious sort of politician, whose peculiarities deserve notice all the more because he was the type and specimen of a class which is fast disappearing from the civilised countries of the world. Inglis represented in the House of Commons the great University of Oxford. He was a man of the highest personal and political integrity and honour; he was a man of education, a man of intellect, an effective speaker; but he was the very bond-slave of Tory prejudice, and the bitter enemy of every measure, large or small, which made for political progress. His name is still well remembered in the House of Commons; some of us can even recall a recollection of the man himself, for his political career lasted a long time and he was a living, walking, speech-making embodiment of antique Toryism. His speech in reply to Lord John Russell was one which ought to have been preserved, if only as a specimen of the kind of argument which could still be employed in the House of Commons by an educated English gentleman who was not supposed to have any tendency to insanity. Indeed, the speech was exactly such a discourse as Sydney Smith might have prepared for the purpose of throwing ridicule on the arguments of the whole Tory Party. Reform he declared to be only revolution under a feigned name. A measure like that introduced by Lord John Russell would root out all the benignant influences of education, property, and rank. Pass such a measure and there would be no more gentlemen and no more scholars in England, and everything in future would be governed there by the caprice of an ignorant and howling mob. He abandoned himself to the spirit of his argument so far as to deny in the most solemn manner that any English law or English custom had ever connected taxation and representation. He went even farther than this; for he insisted that the whole principle of representation was something utterly foreign and unknown to the British constitution. He scoffed at the idea that a place merely because it happened to be a large and prosperous town, with a great population, was any the better entitled to be represented in Parliament than the smallest country village; and he maintained that the principle of representation was that the Sovereign should invite whomsoever he pleased to represent any place, peopled or unpeopled, which the Sovereign graciously chose to designate; and that the man designated should thereupon have the right of going to Parliament, to confer with the Sovereign on the affairs of the country. He went even farther than this; he exceeded even the limits of anything like artistic caricature; for he openly defended and glorified the purchase of small boroughs, and triumphantly pointed out, that if such boroughs were not to be bought and sold then the noblemen of the country, the persons naturally fitted to govern the country, would have no representation whatever in the House of Commons. This was, perhaps, the extreme high-water mark of the most antique Toryism. Sir Robert Inglis naturally defended the system of small boroughs— the rotten boroughs as they came to be called—which were the property of some owner or patron, and were disposed of to anybody whom the patron's good fancy was pleased to favour. He hammered away at this argument with a certain clap-trap effect, when he pointed out that a number of the greatest public men who had adorned the House of Commons could never have had seats there but for the intelligence and generosity of the patrons who discovered their merits, and endowed them with a constituency. We shall presently see that Sir Robert Inglis was not the only man who made use of this argument; that it was used again and again by men far better entitled to a hearing than he; and that it was heard of more than a quarter of a century after the introduction of the first Reform Bill. Sir Robert Inglis then went on to enunciate the proposition dear to the heart of good old Toryism in every country, that everything would be peaceful and happy, if only a flood of mob oratory were not allowed to pour itself all over the land. Mob oratory, with men like Sir Robert Inglis, meant any kind of eloquence which appealed to the hearts and the brains of large numbers of men; and it was an article of faith with him that no human being would ever fancy he had a grievance that ought to be remedied by law, if some mob orator did not get upon an inverted tub and bellow into his ears a story of imaginary wrong. Robert Inglis is dead and gone long ago; but the theory that popular commotion never springs from real grievance, but always comes from the wicked inspirings of irresponsible agitators, is a favourite conviction still with the reactionary party in every country of the world where men form parties at all, and where the patrons of old abuses find their sole enemies in the workings of popular agitation.

Not long after Sir Robert Inglis had finished his speech, a man of a very different order of mind and of eloquence rose to oppose the Ministerial measure of Reform. This was Sir Robert Peel, the second of the name, the great Sir Robert Peel as we may fairly call him. Peel was a Lancashire man; and it is a curious fact that Lancashire has contributed to Parliament the four greatest orators of the present reign : Peel himself, Stanley, afterwards Earl of Derby, Gladstone, and John Bright. Peel's speech against the Reform Bill is said to have been, and we can well believe it, a masterpiece of parliamentary argument. We have to consider what must have been the effect of the noble delivery, the exquisitely chosen language, the appeals skilfully addressed to ingrained prejudice and old-established ideas, in order to understand with what telling force such a speech must have fallen upon the ears of the House of Commons. We have to bear in mind, too, that a distinct majority of those who listened to him were in their secret hearts only too ready to admit the justice of his arguments. But let any reader take up the speech and study it to-day, and the chances are many to one that the first feeling it will arouse in him is one of wonder that a man of Peel's intellect and education could possibly have indulged in such chimeras and believed them to be guiding spirits. Peel began by denouncing all those who had incited the people to a pitch of frenzy, and spurred their lazy indifference until it broke into a revolutionary charge. Peel, one of the most far-seeing and the greatest members of an English Parliament, was in this kind of argument putting himself on an intellectual level with Sir Robert Inglis. According to his contention, the most intelligent Englishman, Irishman, or Scotchman would never have cared whether boroughs were bought or sold, or not ; would never have seen any objection to a deserted plain returning members to Parliament ; or to the Lord of the Manor nominating members to please himself or some of his friends, to reward a parasite, or to please a pretty woman; would never have had the least idea that there was anything wrong, or unconstitutional, or dangerous, or degrading in all this; if only the wicked popular agitators would let him alone, and not try to excite him to delirium. Then came the appeal, which some of my readers have been no doubt already anticipating, the demand how even the wickedest of agitators could be wicked enough to raise such questions at a time when our foreign relations were passing through so profound and grave a crisis. This, of course, is the sort of appeal that is always introduced when any measure of reform is proposed. What! while France is in the throes of a new revolution, is that the time to unsettle our minds by tormenting us about rotten boroughs and unenfranchised millions? "Better a rotten borough or two," sang Tennyson many years later, "than a rotting fleet and towns in flames." Tennyson, however, was a singer, and did not pretend to any knowledge of political affairs, and was not called upon by anybody to explain how the maintenance of the rotten boroughs was to keep a fleet from rotting, and a town from foreign bombardment. Even if the condition of things had been quite different from that which Peel fairly described it to be, Peel might have used his argument just as effectively in another way. He might have asked, Is it at a moment like this, when peace prevails at home and abroad, that you are going to allow your wicked agitators to disturb a nation and a world at rest? Nobody could have known better than Peel did, that the revolution in

France was brought about by the dogged determination of the rulers of that country not to allow any measure of even the most moderate reform. He went over again, although with greater dexterity and effect, the argument of Sir Robert Inglis, in favour of the close borough system. "Consider," he urged, "the number of men who had guided and illumined the House of Commons, and who might never have had a chance of finding a seat there if it were not for the existence of those small close boroughs which the present measure proposed altogether to disfranchise." He ran, indeed, over a glittering bead-roll of names. Burke, Pitt, Fox, Plunket, Canning, Brougham, and many other great men were all returned in the first instance for close boroughs at the nomination of a patron. This same kind of argument was used many years later by Peel's greatest parliamentary successor, Mr. Gladstone. The argument, of course, leaves out of all account the infinite anomalies and abominations which the old system brought with it: the patronage, the bribery, the corruption, the subjection of the nation's best interests to the caprice or the selfish purposes of a few owners of the soil. The fact could not be disputed that there were owners of boroughs here and there generous and enlightened enough to see the merits of men like Burke and Plunket and Canning, and to hand over to them constituencies which they could not possibly have purchased for themselves. But has it ever been shown that a great and populous borough would be in the least degree less likely than a patron or a close corporation to appreciate the gifts of such men, and to give them a chance in the House of Commons? In the England of our time, a new man of great abilities and without money would find a much better chance of a seat in Parliament by addressing himself to some large and populous borough, where the spread of education was telling on the electors, than he would have in some much smaller constituency, where mere local influence and local patronage would be only too likely to carry the day against the stranger.

During the course of the debate, a very remarkable speech was made by the Irish leader, Daniel O'Connell. O'Connell seems to have seen farther and more distinctly into the future than any other of the great orators who took part in the discussion. He declared that he would give the Bill his full support ; but that it was not the sort of measure that he as a Radical reformer would have wished to introduce. The main defect of the Bill, he said, was to be found in the fact that it was not a measure of radical reform. No such measure, he insisted, could ever give abiding satisfaction to the country which did not recognise the principle of universal suffrage ; and he contended that the durations of Parliament ought to be made shorter, and that the votes of the electors ought to be taken by ballot. Already, it has to be observed, we have in Great Britain something nearly approaching to manhood suffrage, and we have vote by ballot, and there is not a reactionary in his senses who believes that the people of these countries could ever be induced to return to the old franchise and the old system of the open vote.

The debate on the first reading was carried on for seven nights. As we have already said, there is very seldom a division taken on the first reading of any measure. The second reading, when it comes on, brings up a debate on the actual principle of the Bill; and a man who votes against the second reading, thereby declares that he disapproves of the whole purpose which the promoters of the Bill have in view. But he may vote for the second reading while firm in the intention to make every alteration he can in the provisions of the Bill as it passes through what is called Committee stage, after second reading, that being the stage at which the Bill comes up for the consideration of all its separate clauses and details. Many a Member of Parliament votes for the second reading of a Bill in the hope that he may so damage it in Committee, as to leave it worth nothing to its promoters. Many observers, themselves hostile to reform, were of opinion then, and many historical writers have been of opinion since, that the Tories made an entire mistake in their way of dealing with the measure. The great difficulty of the Bill, according to these observers and writers, lay, not so much in the House of Commons as outside the House of Commons. Even within the House, as we have already shown, there were many sincere reformers who put up with the Bill rather than welcomed it; who were willing to take it because they were afraid that they could get nothing better just at that time; but who fully shared the opinions of Mr. O'Connell as to the impossibility of its proving adequate to the work of a lasting settlement. Outside the House of Com-

mons the feeling of the Reform Party was much
stronger still. It would have required all the influence
of Lord Grey and Lord John Russell and Lord Durham
and other such men to induce the country to be satisfied with the measure. The opinion, therefore, of the
critics, to whom allusion has been made, was that
the policy of the Tory Opposition would have been
to show no inveterate and determined hostility to the
Bill, to criticise it and censure it, but not to make too
much of it; and let the attention of Reformers outside Parliament be turned rather to the unsatisfactory
character of the measure itself, than to the impassioned and wholesale opposition of the Tories.

It is hardly probable that in any case the Tory
opposition of that day, with men like Sir Robert
Inglis and his friends to urge them on, could have
been capable of any such subtle policy as that which
was recommended to them. But there can be little
doubt that the fury of the Tories went a good way to
make the Bill more popular than it otherwise might
have been. It was almost enough for many of the
Reformers in the country, and especially in the great
towns, to know that the Duke of Wellington and
Lord Sidmouth and Sir Robert Inglis and others
were set against the Bill, in order to make all
true Reformers throw up their caps for it. The
measure had, undoubtedly, two or three splendid
merits. It abolished the principle of nomination to
Parliament by owners or by close corporations; it
established something like a symmetrical system of
voting all over the country; it restored the principle
of representation; and it added about half a million

to the voters of the United Kingdom. But in almost every other of its objects the Reform Bill fell far short of the necessities of the country; and the proof of this is to be found in the number of other Reform Bills that had to be introduced in order to supplement and amend and reconstruct it. The extension of the suffrage was still miserably inadequate; and practically the whole working population of Great Britain and Ireland was left without the chance of a vote—that is without any direct share whatever in the government of the country with which its own dearest interests were bound up. Some of the closing sentences in Lord John Russell's speech were full of an earnest and generous hope as to the result which the measure might have, by stimulating the working classes generally to steady conduct, praiseworthy frugality, and honourable ambition, in order that they might become legally possessed of the quality of citizenship. But the £10 franchise in boroughs and the £50 franchise in counties left hundreds of thousands of honest men without the slightest chance of gratifying their honourable ambitions. Ten pounds a year rent in boroughs, and fifty pounds a year in counties, meant much more money at that time than the same figures would mean now. But even the more advanced Reformers were willing to put up with a good deal of deficiency in order to get a Reform Bill of some kind, which at least established the principle of direct representation. The Reformers out of doors, therefore, welcomed with general enthusiasm the first reading of the Bill; and that first reading was followed at once by the first reading of measures of the same kind for Scotland and for Ireland.

On the 21st of March, 1831, Lord John Russell moved the second reading of the English Reform Bill. The second reading was strongly resisted, and the Tory speakers who had argued against the first reading, declaimed their arguments all over again. Three hundred and two members voted for the second reading, and three hundred and one against it. The second reading, therefore, embodying the whole purpose of the Bill, was carried only by a majority of one. The wildest exultation broke out along the ranks of the Opposition. Every Tory in the House felt satisfied that a Bill which passed its second reading in the House of Commons by only a majority of one would not have the slightest chance of dragging itself through Committee without some mutilation of its principal clauses which would leave it an object of pity to its friends and of ridicule to its enemies. The end of that particular struggle came even sooner than was expected. An amendment proposed by a Tory member, which declared that the number of knights, citizens, and burgesses ought not to be diminished, was opposed by Lord Althorp as fatal to the value of the Bill; and there were two hundred and ninety-nine votes for the amendment and two hundred and ninety-one against it. The Government were, therefore, defeated by a majority of eight votes. There was an end of that particular measure, at all events. Lord Grey and his colleagues were not in the least dismayed. They determined at once to dissolve Parliament and appeal to the country by a General Election, for a reversal of the decision given by the majority of the House of Commons. The first trouble the Ministry had was with the patriot King. William IV. seemed to think it a monstrous thing that he should be asked to dissolve a Parliament which had just been gathered together, after the cost and turmoil of a General Election, only to put the country to the cost and turmoil of another General Election; and all for the sake of carrying a Reform Bill, about which the Sovereign himself felt no manner of personal enthusiasm. On Lord Grey and Lord Brougham, fell the conduct of the negotiations, and Lord Brougham as Keeper of the King's conscience, had to bear the brunt of the more intimate struggle. All sorts of stories were told about the King's efforts at resistance and Lord Brougham's efforts at persuasion; and it had never been supposed by anybody that bland persuasiveness was one of Brougham's endowments. One legend is to the effect that Brougham might never have prevailed over his Sovereign, if it had not been astutely conveyed to the Sovereign's ears, that certain leading Tory Peers had denied to his Majesty any constitutional right of dissolving a Parliament under such conditions. Thereupon, so ran the story, the King declared that if the Peers dared to dispute his prerogative, he would show them that he was determined to exercise it. The story probably is not true, although it found many believers at the time. However, the one thing certain is that the King showed his good sense by allowing himself to be prevailed upon, and he consented to go down to the

House of Lords and declare the Dissolution of the Parliament. Now this, at all events, was recognised by every one as a step in advance of any that would probably have been taken by William's recent predecessors, under similar circumstances; and it gained new credit for the King among the Reformers of the country. Without William's assent the dissolution, of course, could not take place; and therefore the mere announcement that Parliament was to be dissolved was enough to convince all the Reformers of the country that the Sovereign had accepted the views of his constitutional advisers and that William had justified by his action the title of a patriot King. So far as can be guessed the King was pleased by the title; and was hopeful of continuing to deserve it, although he probably could not help wishing every now and then to have a little more of his own way than was permitted to him by the stately and unbending Earl Grey, and the passionate and sometimes blusterous Lord Brougham. The King then gave his consent, and went down to the House of Lords and dissolved the Parliament.

The event was received with tumultuous delight in London, and in nearly all the great towns, and indeed all over the country. London was illuminated, and so were most of the large provincial cities. Unfortunately the exultations were accompanied by a certain degree of violence. In the West-end of London many of the opponents of Reform refused to put lights in their windows, and the windows of such recusants were smashed by a roaring crowd. Apsley House, the town residence of the Duke of

Wellington, has a side row of windows which look into Hyde Park. There was a noisy demonstration outside the house, and the Hyde Park windows were all smashed to pieces. The Duke of Wellington's own comment on the event was that the demonstration of hostility ought to have taken place—it was then the month of June—on the fifteenth of that month, the day of the crowning victory of Waterloo. "That day he overcame the Nervii," is the heart-thrilling line in which Shakespeare's Mark Antony tells how the wound of the assassin's dagger came in Cæsar's mantle; in that mantle which he put on for the first time on a summer's evening in his tent after his victory. The Duke of Wellington was probably not a great student of Shakespeare, and in any case he was not egotistic enough to think of applying to himself the words that related to Julius Cæsar; but the application might have been made for all that. The mob, however, did no great harm and did not mean to do much harm. They broke the unlighted windows as a London mob of June, 1897, might possibly, without meaning much harm, have broken some windows kept ostentatiously dark, on the night of the Queen's Jubilee Celebration. But the Duke, undoubtedly, took the insult to heart; and for some years the windows that turned on the Park were kept rigidly shuttered. When the Election began, the contest was kept up on both sides with an utter prodigality of expense. There was not much to be said in favour of one side against the other, so far as bribery and corruption were concerned. Bribery and corruption ran their unblushing way among

Liberals and Tories, throughout nearly all the constituencies. As the results began to be known, it was found that nearly all the cities and great towns were on the side of Lord Grey and Lord John Russell. One of the most conspicuous opponents of the Reform Bill was turned out of the important town of Liverpool by an immense majority of votes. Many of the counties had likewise "gone solid" for Reform, to use a phrase familiar in modern politics. There was no mistaking the meaning of all this; the feeling of the country was distinctly in favour of Reform. The new Parliament was opened on June 21st by William IV. in person; and as the King went in state to the House of Lords, he was received with immense enthusiasm by the crowds who thronged the streets. William enjoyed the enthusiasm very much, and was more than ever satisfied of his just claim to the title of patriot King.

X

THE REFORM BILL AGAIN

ON the 24th of June Lord John Russell introduced a second Reform Bill which might be called just the same in principle and substance as that which he had brought in on the former occasion. The second reading was moved for on the 4th of July; and after a debate of three nights a division was taken, and the second reading was carried by three hundred and sixty-seven votes for, and two hundred and thirty-one against—a majority of one hundred and thirty-six in favour of the principle of the measure. This put an end to all hope on the part of the Tories that anything could be done in the way of direct opposition to the Reform Bill. But now the Tories put into action for the first time, on a great and systematic scale, those tactics of parliamentary obstruction which have become so familiar to the political world in more modern days. The forms of the House of Commons then, and even to a much later time, afforded infinite opportunities for the reckless ingenuity of Tory members to find means of postponing and postponing any chance of coming to a decision upon anything. It will be interesting to give some illustration of the manner in which this system of interruption was kept up without actually violating any of the rules of order which govern the proceedings of the House. For instance, what could be more reasonable than for any member who thought the House had sat and debated long enough on that particular subject, to rise and move that the House do now adjourn? Every sitting of the House is brought to a close by a motion couched in just such a form, which on all ordinary occasions and at a reasonable hour of the night, is agreed to without discussion or division. But in the instances we are describing a member who moves that the House do now adjourn, had not the slightest desire that the question should be put to an instant division; he wanted all the debate that he could have; he wanted to help in wearing the Government out. Therefore, he gave all the reasons that occurred to him, all that his uttermost ingenuity could devise, to show that the House was bound to adjourn just then, and he gave his reasons at immense length; and went over them again and again as if he had taken all time for his province. In Sir Philip Sidney's "Arcadia" we are told of a beautiful young shepherd-boy who stands under the trees on some fair summer's evening piping as though he should never grow old. There is something charming in the idea of this young lover of music, piping on and on, as though youth and harmony were to be always his own. The Conservative orator talked in favour of an adjournment as though he should never grow old, as though he had all time before him; but his was not quite so picturesque a figure as that drawn by Sir Philip Sidney. When one Conservative orator had finished his speech, another Conservative orator took up the tale, and yet another, and another; until at last it was thought to be convenient for a division to be taken. The majority, of course, voted for going on with the business and making some progress with the Reform Bill, and the motion for adjournment was therefore defeated. But the Tory tactics endured, and a moment after the division had been declared some Tory member got up and moved that the Speaker do now leave the Chair, which was only another way of getting rid of the Bill for that sitting. Then came another long debate and another division; and the Tories being once more defeated, some Tory member fell back on the old motion that the House do now adjourn. This was in strict accordance with the rules, which did not allow precisely the same motion to be moved twice in succession; and so the alternate motions that the House do now adjourn, and that the Speaker do leave the Chair, were kept up until breakfast time in the morning, and then the members were allowed to go to their homes, having to meet again at three that afternoon. For day after day and night after night this sort of thing went on. Nobody in the House listened to the debates, nobody outside the house paid the slightest attention to what the Tories were saying.

The one question of keen public interest was how long the Government could hold out against this peculiar kind of opposition. It might be taken for granted that after a certain period in the year it would be all but impossible to keep the House of Commons together; even the most earnest Reformers had other duties to discharge besides waiting for the divisions on the motion that the House do now adjourn. Many of Lord Grey's followers began to be seriously afraid that the whole session might be wasted without advancing the Reform scheme in any measurable degree towards success. The Government, however, held firm; and the disfranchisement of what were called the rotten boroughs was absolutely accomplished so far as the House of Commons could accomplish it. Then came the struggle over the reduction in the representation of various boroughs from two members to one member. Hereupon the obstruction got up again, alive and fully armed for the work. The methods of obstruction had by this time been organised and arranged as by a regular process of drill. It is well to learn something on this subject from Mr. Molesworth's excellent "History of the Reform Bill." Mr. Molesworth tells us—and the facts are indeed beyond dispute—that there was a regular division of labour in the work of obstruction, arranged and superintended by a Committee of which Sir Robert Peel was Chairman. Now we have had a good deal of obstruction, deliberate and purposed obstruction, in the House of Commons in later days; but it never happened since 1831 that a statesman of the rank of Sir Robert Peel became President of a Committee for the express and the sole purpose of arranging and supplying a mere obstruction by speech-making, to prevent a popular measure from passing on its way through the House of Commons. The same arguments were repeated over and over again without the slightest pretence of a desire to find something new. Sir Robert Peel himself set a good example to his comrade obstructionists. During one stage of the debate he delivered no less than forty-eight speeches. Mr. Wilson Croker, a literary critic whom Macaulay made famous by his scathing essay and who was for a long time, when Secretary to the Admiralty, the target for some of Lord Cochrane's most dashing and bitter attacks—Mr. Wilson Croker spoke fifty-seven times. Sir Charles Wetherell, who has been already mentioned in this history as a type of Tory of the extinct school, went one speech better, for he spoke fifty-eight times.

In the meantime, the reformers of the country were not idle. Meetings were held in London, and in most of the towns, calling on the Government to take heart of grace, and not to give in to the Tories by a single inch; but to keep Parliament sitting until the Bill should have gone through its every stage. The Government answered pluckily to these appeals. A meeting of influential supporters of the Ministry was held in the Foreign Office; and to that meeting Lord Althorp declared on behalf of his colleagues, that the enemies of Reform would find themselves miserably mistaken. Rather than abandon the Bill, he assured his hearers, Parliament would be kept sitting until the next December or the next December twelvemonths if necessary. That settled the opposition for the moment. Amendments were still proposed and debates still went on, and divisions were taken; but the Tories began to see at last that the Government were thoroughly in earnest, and that the country was behind Lord Grey and Lord John Russell. The Bill was carried through its various stages, and the last division on the motion, that the Bill do now pass, showed three hundred and forty-five votes for the Reform measure, and only two hundred and thirty-nine against it—a majority of one hundred and six in favour of the Bill.

Then the hopes and hearts of all the Anti-reformers turned to the House of Lords. The House of Lords had then, as now, a large Conservative majority, and had, therefore, the power of upsetting the work of the Commons, and rejecting the Reform Bill altogether. There are two checks on the unlimited exercise of such a power by the House of Lords; the one constitutional, and the other political and moral. The constitutional check is found in the fact that the Sovereign has always the right, on the advice of his Ministers, to create as many new Peers as he thinks fit. If, therefore, there should be in the House of Lords a known majority of Peers, say one hundred in number, against Reform, the King would only have to create one hundred and fifty new Peers from the Liberal ranks in time to carry the Reform measure through all its stages. Of course, this is what might be called a desperate remedy; and could only be tried as a last resource. With a Sovereign like George III. it never could be tried, because the King would never give his consent to a wholesale creation of Peers for such a purpose. In any case, only the most extreme emergency could induce a

Liberal Ministry to have recourse to such a constitutional device. It was one of the many devices which may be called into existence under the British constitution; and which yet appear to be in themselves fantastically unconstitutional and anomalous. Therefore the Tories felt in good confidence that Lord Grey would not advise the Sovereign to take so unusual and extraordinary a step; and that William IV., no matter how many crowds might have called him the patriot King, would never adopt that way of showing his patriotic sentiment. The other check on the power of the House of Lords was that created by the strength of popular feeling out of doors. If the majority of the constituencies should prove themselves so determined on Reform that the prolonged resistance of the Peers might risk a revolution, then it was almost certain that the House of Lords would give way and yield to the popular will. Such a result has always come about in recent years. The House of Lords in our times may be relied upon never to resist the demands of the constituencies so far as to lead to a crisis which might end in the overthrow of the hereditary chamber itself. We have grown used to that condition of things lately; and curiously enough the fact serves as an argument to those who are in favour of the present constitution of the House of Lords, and to those who are determinedly against it. The advocates of the House of Lords ask the country what serious objection there can be to a chamber which, at the most, can only interpose delay and allow fuller time for calm consideration; and they point to the fact that the House

of Lords have never driven their opposition to any
dangerous extent, or done aught to provoke revolutionary demands. On the other hand, the opponents
of the House of Lords ask what can be the use of
an institution which does not any longer even profess
to be a saviour of society; which has long since
renounced every pretence at a mission to save society
from society's self; and is always ready to give way
if society only makes clamour enough to be accepted
as a danger-signal. In the days of the First Reform
Bill, however, the resisting power of the House of
Lords to any popular movement had not been
thoroughly tested; and the Tories in general were
of good hope that the Lords would hold out, that
the King would hold out, and that the mob orators
and anarchists would have to slink back into the
state of obscurity to which it had pleased Providence
to call them. The Tory Peers kept up for awhile
their show of a resolute purpose. On October
3rd, Lord Grey moved the second reading of the
Reform Bill; Lord Wharncliffe moved as an amendment, that the Bill be read a second time that day
six months, a motion which amounted to the rejection
of the measure. The Duke of Wellington spoke, as
was to be expected, uncompromisingly against the
Bill; Lord Lyndhurst, one of the greatest lawyers
of his day, opposed it more dexterously, but not less
decidedly; Lord Brougham thundered in its favour.
The division was taken on the morning of October
8th; and it was announced that the second reading
was defeated by a majority of forty-one. The
House of Commons had spent a whole session

in vain over the passing of the Reform Bill; the House of Lords undid the work in a few days. Yet the majority against the measure was not after all so great as might have been expected, and some of the Peers who had voted in the majority must have felt themselves wondering as they went home that morning, whether they had not hastened, rather than retarded, the movement of Reform.

The news of the adverse division in the House of Lords created a passionate sensation all over the country. Great meetings were held in every city and town; in many places the shops were closed and mourning bells were pealed from some of the churches. One of the most popular ideas of the day was the suggested expedient that a run should be made upon the Bank of England for gold, with the view of obstructing the whole movement of commerce, in the hope that thereby the Lords might be brought to their senses; and a run for gold was actually made, which at one time created much alarm. In the streets from Charing Cross to the Houses of Parliament vast crowds assembled every evening, cheering the leaders of the Reform movement, and hissing and cursing the Peers or Commoners who had opposed the Bill. Clamorous proposals for the abolition of the House of Lords became popular on every Radical platform all over the country; serious riots took place at Derby, at Nottingham, and at Bristol; the castles and country houses of Tory noblemen and squires were attacked, seriously damaged, and in some instances set on fire. One instance of this form of riot is worth a special mention, if only because of the curious and touching poetic associations which it brings up with it. The house of Mr. Musters, near Nottingham, was set on fire. Mr. Musters was the husband of the Mary Chaworth, who in the days of our fathers and grandfathers was dear to every sentimental heart, as Lord Byron's first love, about whom he wrote his famous poem, "The Dream." When the house was set on fire, Mrs. Musters, Mary Chaworth, fled in alarm and found refuge for awhile in one of the gardens. The terror and the cold night air proved too much for her, and she caught an attack of illness which ended soon after in her death.

Many of the Reformers were even impatient of Lord Grey and Lord John Russell themselves. An impression got abroad somehow, that the Government might be disposed to tamper with the people by yielding so far to the House of Lords as to consent to a postponement of the Reform Bill. The bare surmise or suspicion was enough for a time to bring a certain amount of unpopularity on the heads of the leading Ministers. In truth, the country was aflame with passion; and a rash act or two, even perhaps a rash word or two, on either side of the political field, might have brought about a tumult, which would have seemed to distant eyes not altogether unlike a popular revolution. It can never be known for certain how near England really did come at that crisis to a genuine revolutionary struggle. Looking back upon that time, with only the experience of more recent days to guide our judgment, it is easy enough to tell ourselves complacently that nothing serious could have occurred, that the English are a steadfast people, little like the French and foreigners generally, and not in the least addicted to revolution; and that everything would have worked out quietly for the best. History tells us that the English people have never shown themselves afraid to risk a revolution when there seemed no other means of removing an intolerable grievance and making it sure that national justice must be done. The more we study the records of that Reform time, the more we shall be inclined to believe that England was brought very near indeed to revolution. How far were the more influential leaders of the Liberal Party aware of the threatening danger, and what thoughts were passing through their minds as to the preparations that would have to be made, in order to encounter it? That, of course, we shall never fully know. But it is at least certain that some of those leaders must have found their minds perplexed by the doubt whether the King would yield to, or would resist, the advice of the Ministry and the demands of the country; and if he should decide upon resistance, what was to happen next? Were the Liberal leaders to allow things to drift into mere tumult, or were they not to take some steps which might provide for the guidance of the people and secure the country against the worst? Suppose the King were to set himself doggedly against the advice of his Ministers and were to declare that he would throw in his own fate, and that of his dynasty, with the action of the House of Lords; what would remain to be done in such a case? The question must have come up to the mind of many a statesman of that time—whether in such a case it would be the duty of the great Liberal nobles of England to side with the King against the House of Commons and the people, or to stand as their forefathers did, with the Parliament —that is, with the real Parliament, and against the revolutionary action of the Crown. The dilemma, says a recent writer, appeared not unlike that which was presented when Charles I. broke away from his Parliament; and he adds, that some at least of the influential English nobles seemed to have been inclined to cast in their lot with the Parliament, and against the Sovereign, in the event of the Sovereign proving faithless to the constitutional principles by virtue of which alone he held his Crown. Such a condition of things appears almost incredible to us now. We have so long been accustomed to the steady and safe working of the political system under a thoroughly constitutional Sovereign, that we find it hard to realise the possibility of a crisis occurring at so recent a date, which would have rendered it necessary for great English noblemen to make up their minds as to which side was that of revolution, and which side was that of the constitution. But it is quite certain that such a question was presented for decision to some of the great Liberal nobles. Suppose the country were to be thrown into actual domestic strife by the possible action of the Sovereign, that action being a breach of the constitution, on which side were the defenders of law and order to take their stand? It came out, during the course of a great political trial some sixteen years afterwards, that a correspondence had been opened, undoubtedly under the sanction of some of the great Reformers, with Sir Charles Napier, the famous soldier, for the purpose of endeavouring to secure beforehand the co-operation of the army, should the worst come to the worst. It is not too much to say, that for some time England was trembling on the very verge of a revolution.

Parliament was called together again, on December 6, 1831. The King opened the session in person, and announced in his Royal Speech that Bills would be introduced for the Reform of the House of Commons, with the added declaration, that the speedy and satisfactory settlement of this question becomes daily of more pressing importance to the security of the State and the contentment and the welfare of the people. It was possibly thought by the leading Ministers, that this emphatic declaration might have the effect of discouraging the leaders of the Opposition, and teaching them that in the opinion of the King himself, the time had gone by for any further resistance to Reform. The words, however, had no such effect. The leaders of the Tory Party were convinced in their hearts that the King was opposed to the Ministerial proposals for Reform, and that he was only waiting for an opportunity to throw cold water upon the whole agitation. On the other hand, the Reformers out of doors still cherished the opinion that the King was in favour of Reform, and that he was prepared to go any constitutional length which the advice of his Ministers could suggest. On the 12th of December, Lord John Russell moved in the

GENERAL SIR CHARLES JAMES NAPIER, G.C.B.
(1782–1853.)

House of Commons for leave to bring in his third Reform Bill. The Bill was in all important details, and of course in all its principles, much the same as the first and second Bills. The first reading passed without a division; and when the second reading came on there were three hundred and twenty-four votes for the Bill, and one hundred and sixty-two against it; so that the supporters of the measure were now in a majority of exactly two to one over their opponents. Then Parliament adjourned for the Christmas holidays. Part of the sacred and gladsome season was occupied in the trial of the rioters who had been arrested for creating disturbances throughout the country. Those were stern times, and the unfortunate rioters received in many cases the hardest punishment the law could inflict. There were four executions of rioters at Bristol, and three at Nottingham. Parliament came together again on the 17th of January, 1832; and on January 20th the House of Commons went into Committee on the Reform Bill. Then the work of obstruction came on with fresh vigour. The Bill did not get through Committee until March 14th; and it passed its third reading by a majority of one hundred and sixteen, on the 23rd of the month. It was sent up to the House of Lords at once; and then two popular questions at once arose which have been echoed and re-echoed often since that time.

The first question was, What will the House of Lords do with the Bill? and the second, and more ominous question, was, What is to be done with the House of Lords? Now, by this time, there had been formed amongst the Peers a sort of third party, who became popularly known as the "Waverers," just as in former days another political party had been known by the name of the "Trimmers." The Waverers consisted for the most part, if not altogether, of men who were opposed to the Reform Bill, and, indeed, to all comprehensive schemes of Reform; but who, nevertheless, were not prepared to push their Conservatism to dangerous lengths. These men were for staving off reform as long as they could, but they were not willing to run the risk of a social convulsion in their anxiety to defeat or delay the Ministerial measure. They saw clearly enough that the crisis was becoming most serious and important; and probably their uttermost hopes at this stage of the proceedings were limited to the possibility of reducing the Reform Bill to what they would have considered a comparatively harmless measure. The student of English history will be interested in observing the fact that every great struggle for political reform in England developes in one or both Houses of Parliament, a third party which contrives to get into its hands for the time the balance of power, and thus become masters of the situation. In most instances the third party is formed by Liberals who fall away from their leaders on some project of reform, and are ready to give their votes and their help to the anti-reform opposition. In the Reform movement of 1831 the third party was composed of men who, being anti-reformers themselves, were yet willing to use the power they had got on the side of a Reform measure, rather than run the risk of a popular uprising. The fact, however, remains the same; and students who want to get at a thorough understanding of our modern history must take account of it, that every struggle between political progress and political reaction in England calls into existence a third party who contrive for the hour to get into their hands the key of the situation. To the Waverers, therefore, the eyes of most people turned as the possessors of the way out of the deadlock. It was quite certain that if Lord Grey could induce the King to give his consent to the creation of new Peers in sufficient number, the Waverers would never think of putting Sovereign or Government to the trouble of carrying any such measure into effect. The mere announcement that the King had given his consent would be enough for them; and they would at once withdraw from further opposition to the Reform Bill. Of what avail would it be for the Waverers to carry their opposition any farther? If the King chose to create new Peers out of the Liberal ranks in sufficient number to form a majority for the passing of the Bill what could the Waverers get by resistance? The Bill would be carried in any case; and they would only have the discomfort and the humiliation of seeing their hereditary chamber flooded by a number of Liberals from all parts of the country, who had suddenly, at the King's order, been converted into Peers, and who could go on passing further and further Reforms of all kinds for the remainder of their natural lives. The Waverers, in fact, hoped that by standing out to a certain extent against the Bill they might strengthen the King in his supposed determination not to create new Peers; while the King, for his part, was still, no doubt, under the impression that the Waverers might frighten the Ministry so far as to induce them to leave out of their measure the principles which the King thought harmful, but which the people ardently desired to establish. The King, therefore, delayed and delayed; and Lord Grey could not obtain any promise from him.

The Bill came on for second reading in the House of Lords on 9th of April, and the Duke of Wellington spoke out as strongly against the measure as he had spoken against the First Reform Bill brought in by the Government. He was, however, much more indiscreet in this speech than he had been on the former occasion, and he went so far as to declare his conviction, that the King himself was not in favour of any such measure of Reform as his Ministers were endeavouring to force upon the House of Lords. The Duke, indeed, exceeded himself in his indiscretion on this occasion; for he declared his full belief, that if the King's real feelings only could be made known to the country, Lord Grey would never have the slightest chance of passing such a measure as that which he had been reckless enough to introduce to Parliament. The Waverers, however, were not altogether satisfied with the rash declarations of the Duke of Wellington, and they supported the second reading, and thus enabled the reading to be carried by a majority of nine. Thus they satisfied their purpose and their policy by enabling the Government to carry their measure another stage; while, at the same time, making it clear to the Opposition that if the Government refused to give way on some material points, the Bill could be so mutilated by the help of the Waverers as to make it utterly unsatisfactory to the country. Accordingly, the Waverers gave the next helping hand to the Opposition. Lord Lyndhurst proposed an amendment which the Government properly declared to be hostile to the conduct of the Bill; and the Waverers supported Lord Lyndhurst, and his motion was carried by a majority of thirty-five. Lord Grey at once addressed himself to the King, and as the King still hesitated about granting him the power to make new Peers, Lord Grey instantly tendered his resignation. The resignation was accepted; indeed, there was nothing to be done but to accept it, or to give in to Lord Grey's demands King William knew well that when Lord Grey had once made up his mind it would be useless for even the Sovereign to attempt any argument or persuasion with him. Lord Grey and his colleagues went out of office; and the King was left, metaphorically, face to face with the country, face to face with the possibility of revolution. The King sent for Lord Lyndhurst, and pathetically, perplexedly, besought for help and counsel. Lord Lyndhurst had only one piece of advice to give, the only piece of advice any Tory could have given under the circumstances, and that was to send for the Duke of Wellington. The Duke was sent for; and the King implored him to undertake the formation and the leadership of a new Government. The Duke of Wellington had encountered many terrible risks and difficulties in his time; but he had never encountered any risk or any difficulty when there was not the slightest chance of any good purpose whatever being served by the attempt. He told the King bluntly that he did not believe it would be possible for him to get together any Government which could face the crisis; and in order not to be wanting in advice of some kind, he recommended the King to send for Sir Robert Peel, and try what Peel could do. Then, and for ever after, while Peel's life lasted, the Duke of Wellington looked up to Peel with a genuine and a generous admiration as the man who could do anything, if anything was possible to be done. So the King sent for Peel; but Peel saw that this was a case in which he could do nothing. Peel was one of the most rising men of the time. He must have known that he had a great career before him; and he was quite unselfish and patriotic enough to think little of risking that career, if only thereby something could be done to serve the Sovereign and the State. But he was an intensely practical man, and he did not see that either Sovereign or State could be served by his simply dashing his head against a stone wall. So he told the King that it would be utterly impossible for him to keep together a Ministry against the House of Commons and against the country, and he declined to attempt the impossible task. Then the King in despair sent for the Duke of Wellington again and made it something like a point of duty and of loyalty with him to help the Sovereign out of his dilemma. The Duke, who never was, and never could be, a politician, was willing after such an appeal to dash his head against the stone wall, and so he did actually attempt to get together an administration composed of men who would stand up with him as opponents of Reform, the House of Commons, and the country. The attempt utterly failed. Indeed, to say that it failed is to give an inadequate idea of its futility. No sooner was it made than it had to be abandoned. There were no men outside Bedlam who would undertake to co-operate in such a task.

What was the poor bewildered King to do? He could think of nothing, and nothing could be suggested to him but to send for Lord Grey again, and request Lord Grey to reconstruct his Ministry and go on with the Reform Bill. While all this was happening the public mind was growing more and more furious and the popularity of the patriot King had entirely gone under. William was now denounced every day and every night in the streets of London, and through all the great towns of England, Ireland, and Scotland. When his carriage was seen in the West-end streets of London it became instantly surrounded by hooting, hissing, fist-shaking mobs. Indeed, the poor Sovereign had to be most carefully guarded in order to secure him against the possibility of some direct personal attack. Now King William was a brave man, and an honest man; and we may be sure that he did not take any account of the personal danger; but he had enjoyed the popularity which came around him of late years, and it pained him to find himself an object of distrust and dislike to so large a proportion of his subjects. What course but one was left for him to pursue? He had no taste for the stirring up of a popular revolution; and amongst those to whom he looked for advice he found no trustworthy person who could counsel him to any such purpose. Wellington,

Lyndhurst, Peel, could not help him out of his difficulty; he had to go back to Lord Grey, and Lord Grey was inexorable. Nothing was to be done unless William would give his consent to the creation of new Peers. Lord Brougham, who accompanied Lord Grey in one momentous interview with the Sovereign, went so far as to insist that the consent must even be given in writing. The poor King had no other course open to him than to yield to stern necessity. He had argued with the inexorable long enough; and he was thoroughly tired of the futile argument. He gave his consent, and he gave it even in writing. "The King grants permission to Lord Grey and to his Chancellor, Lord Brougham, to create such a number of Peers as will insure the passing of the Reform Bill," were the words of the consent written on the paper which the King, at last submissive, handed to the rigorous and uncourtly Lord Brougham.

Of course, the moment the consent was given the crisis was all over. It is needless to say that the new Peers were never created. It was enough for the Opposition to know that the new Peers would be created if necessary, and there was an end of their resistance at once. They did not want the Reform Bill, and they did not want the new Peers; but, above all things, they did not want the Reform Bill and the new Peers together. The Duke of Wellington and some other Peers withdrew from the House of Lords altogether while the Bill was running its now short and summary course. They would not look upon the consummation of a policy which it was not possible for them any longer to retard. The

Waverers gave way and the fight was over. On the 4th of June the Bill passed through the House of Lords; and a few days after the poor patriot King had given it his Royal Assent.

Let us see now what were the two great precedents, the two great principles which were established by the passing of the Reform Bill, and by the manner in which it passed into law. We have already told our readers what the Bill itself did for the country; we have described the general reforms which it created; and we have shown in what measure it was seriously defective; and why it became necessary that many further expansions of its scope should be brought about. But the great principles accomplished by the passing of the Reform Bill are not to be found embodied in the contents of the Bill itself. The most important constitutional principles established for the first time, and we trust for all time, by the triumph of Lord Grey and Lord John Russell are two in number. The first is, that the House of Lords must never carry resistance to any measure coming from the House of Commons, that is, from the chamber which represents the country, beyond the point at which it becomes evident that the House of Commons is in earnest, and that the country is behind it. It is now settled that the House of Lords shall have no greater power of resistance to a popular measure than that which, in a different form, is given to the President of the United States, the power to delay its passing until the House of Commons shall have had full time to reconsider its decision and say, on that reconsideration, whether it is of the same mind as before, or not. Many English Reformers think that even this degree of power is far too much to be given to the House of Lords as at present constituted; but it is not necessary to enter into that question. It is enough to say, that since the passing of the Reform Bill, the House of Lords has never, for any considerable length of time, put itself in direct antagonism to the House of Commons. The second great principle which the passing of the Reform Bill established is, that the Sovereign of England must give way to the advice of his Ministers on any question of vital import to the State, and that the personal authority of the Monarch is no longer to decide the course of the Government. Never, since that time, has the personal will of the Sovereign been exercised as a decisive force to contradict and counteract the resolve of the House of Commons. The country is happy, indeed, which has seen so beneficent a change accomplished, and to all appearance safely accomplished for ever, without the need of recourse to revolution.

It might have been worth a revolution to effect such a change, if it could be accomplished by no other means. For the peaceful results we must thank the people of these countries, we must thank the patriotic Ministers like Lord Grey and Lord John Russell, we must thank the House of Commons, and, let it be added, that some thanks are also due to the King, who had the manhood not to be afraid of submitting his personal feelings and wishes to the better judgment of his Ministers and to the welfare of the country. Looking back composedly, at this distance of time, and after the experience of many succeeding Reform Bills, it seems surprising to most of us that the Conservative Party did not better understand the real strength of the movement which they were striving to resist. It seems hard to comprehend how they could have looked at the condition of things which prevailed just before the Reform Bill was introduced, the parliamentary representation of empty spaces, the right of the landowner and the close corporation to nominate anybody to the House of Commons whom the landlord or the close corporation thought fit to honour with patronage, the close boroughs, the rotten boroughs, the open and unabashed system of bribery and corruption, the seats bought and sold like goods at an auction; it seems hard to comprehend how any intelligent Conservative could have looked at things as they were and not have seen for himself that such things could not possibly last. There were intelligent Conservatives in those days, as in all days. The Conservative Party had men of intellect, men even of genius, among their leading members. They had Peel, they had Lyndhurst, they had many other men who might have been capable of guiding a party aright at such a crisis; they had before them the example of the United States, where the Colonies achieved their independence after a tremendous struggle, rather than endure a system of government without adequate representation; they had seen the historic monarchy of France overturned, because the people would no longer submit to be governed by the will of the Sovereign; they had only just seen how another monarchy, set up in France by the combined strength of all the great European Powers, had been upset because the people found no proper representation in the political system. They might have known that the people of these countries are not patient to servility, and that the days of personal government—government by the caprice of the Sovereign—were gone for ever. They might even have observed that the Reform Bill, brought in by Lord Grey and Lord John Russell, did not by any means satisfy the desires of the most earnest Reformers outside and inside Parliament. They might have seen that the Reform Bill as it stood was only possible because so many influential Reform leaders were willing to come to terms of compromise with Lord Grey, and to accept half a loaf because it was better than no bread. Under such conditions it may well seem surprising to us now, that the Conservatives should not have seen the palpable fact that Reform of some kind must come, and that Lord Grey's scheme was the most moderate which the country could possibly accept. But the impression of the Conservatives up to the last moment seems to have been, that if only they could defeat Lord Grey and his Reform Bill the whole question would be settled, and that nothing more would be heard of Reform for many generations to come. On the whole, these countries have no reason to regret that the Tories fought out their battle to the end; and that they brought the King face to face with the question, whether to submit his personal will or to risk a revolution. If they had compromised with Lord Grey, the principle of government by the will of the Sovereign might have dragged on for a few years more, and the battle might have been fought under leaders less capable than Lord Grey and Lord John Russell.

The name of Lord John Russell reminds us that in one of the closing debates on the Reform Bill in the House of Commons, Russell made use of a particular phrase which was afterwards brought up against him many times. The more extreme Reformers found fault with the phrase because they thought it showed, on Russell's part, a lack of earnestness in the cause of Reform, indeed, a lack of true understanding as to the meaning of Reform; while the anti-Reformers used it as an argument to prove that the Government had pledged the Liberal Party to be content with the way it had already made, and to seek no further progress. Lord John Russell said, that "so far as Ministers were concerned, the Reform Bill was, in his opinion, a final measure." It was at once assumed by the extreme men on both sides, that Lord John Russell, on the part of the Government, meant to declare that enough had been done in the way of Reform, that the country had had all the Reform it wanted or could get; that no further steps were to be taken in any similar direction, and that the Reform Bill of 1832 was final. Lord John Russell undoubtedly gave a good chance, by his phrase, to those on the one side who thought his Reform Bill inadequate, and to those on the other side who thought that the most limited scheme of Reform would be far too much. We all understand now quite well what Lord John Russell meant;

although it certainly would have been better if he had made his meaning more clear at the time. Most assuredly it never entered into a mind like that of Lord John Russell to believe that the Reform Bill which he and his colleagues had carried would satisfy the growing political wants of the people of England for all time. A man like Lord John Russell must have known very well, Lord John Russell of course did know very well, that the £50 franchise in counties and the £10 franchise in boroughs could not satisfy the needs of an ever-growing population. No man of Russell's intellect could have supposed for a moment that the whole working population of England could be content to remain for ever without that political franchise which was already given to the people of France and the people of the American Republic. What Russell meant clearly was that the Government had completed for the present their chapter of Reform. No man knew better than Lord John Russell did, that the people of these countries are not likely to devote all their days to political agitation; and that when they have accomplished one triumph in the way of Reform, they will be found ready to return to their ordinary pursuits, and to wait until some new exigency brings about the necessity of accomplishing another work of the same kind. Russell, in fact, continued during all the rest of his long political career, to be as earnest an advocate of Reform as he had proved himself to be, when for the first time he introduced his Reform Bill—for it may well be called his—to the House of Commons. His name was identified with many another project of Reform, with Reform schemes launched by him in later days, and carried to success by him or by others who acted on his inspiration. But he spoke the words of plain common sense when he said that the Government of Lord Grey believed they had done their work for the time in carrying their Reform Bill and were free, if they thought well, to stand aside and leave future work to future hands.

The close of the great debates on the Reform Bill may be regarded also as, in one sense, the close of a great career. Here Charles, Earl Grey, to quote the words of Carlyle applied to Mirabeau, "drops from the tissue of our history, not without a tragic farewell." Lord Grey had a special work appointed for him to do; and he did it, patiently, perseveringly, and with success. From the distant days when he had presented the petition of "the friends of the people" to the House of Commons, from those days, and indeed from days long before, Lord Grey had been a steady and devoted friend of Reform. He had followed the guidance of Fox, although he had little of Fox's enthusiasm or of that gleam of the poetic and the romantic which inspired so much of Fox's eloquence. Lord Grey was by descent, by position, and by temperament, an aristocrat of the aristocrats; and it would not have been under ordinary circumstances natural for him to concern himself much about securing the franchise for a class of men with whom in most cases he could have little or nothing in common. A political rival of Mirabeau once said that Mirabeau owed much of his success to his "terrible gift of familiarity," his power of entering into the ways and feelings and common talk of men of the humblest class. Grey had none of that terrible gift of familiarity; he could not talk to people in general, he was cold and austere among men even of his own class, he was sometimes almost tongue-tied when he had to deal with unlettered strangers. It stands all the more to his honour that he fought the great Reform battle so chivalrously, that he ordered his brave soul to face the struggle, and that he faced it until success came in the end. Lord Grey was the last English Minister who had served on anything like terms of equality with such men as Pitt, and Fox, and Burke, and Sheridan. Macaulay says well of him that "those who had listened to his stately eloquence in the House of Lords, could all the better understand what that group of men must have been among whom he was not the foremost."

XI

SLAVERY—BLACK AND WHITE

THE first great work done by the Reformed Parliament was the total abolition of Slavery in the West Indian and other colonies of England. The new Parliament, indeed, showed itself very eager for the work of reform in any and every direction, and we shall presently see with what energy and success it applied itself to its very various tasks. If anything were needed to prove that a great modern nation makes progress in proportion to the genuineness of its representative system, such proof would be amply furnished by the history of the first Reformed Parliament. The reform in the representative system had not, indeed, gone nearly as far as was needed or as it was destined before very long to go; but it had gone far enough to make it certain that a Parliament which is brought directly in touch of public opinion is able to do great work, even under reluctant or lukewarm sovereigns. The new Parliament applied itself at this very period of its history to the abolition of the odious slavery system which still prevailed in many of the English

Colonies. The slave trade system had been put down long before; that is, so far as English influence and the strength of English navies could put it down. Even at the present day the slave trade lingers here and there, and shows itself by fits and starts, although all the civilised nations of the world are now in arms against it. England had at one time, it must be owned, been herself a sad offender in the toleration and the actual practice of the slave trade. But better times had come, and England had repented of her former error, and had done her very best to suppress the unnatural traffic. Still it was quite a different task to attempt the abolition of the system of domestic slavery in Colonies where that system had existed from time immemorial. England took over her Colonies burdened with the slavery system; and had not, it must be said, concerned herself very much with any persistent efforts to get rid of the odious institution.

There had, indeed, been for a long time growing up in England a party of philanthropic reformers, whose main purpose was to relieve the English Colonies from the shame and the sin of slavery. Brougham was one of the most eloquent and energetic of the men whose voice had always denounced the slave system. It was he who, in energetic and memorable words, cried out against "the wild and guilty fantasy that man can hold property in man." Zachary Macaulay, the father of the famous historian, had taken a most active and enlightened part in the movement for the suppression of the slave system. He had himself given practical evidence of his sincerity, at the same time that he had accumulated an immense amount of knowledge which he put at the service of those who were endeavouring to arouse public opinion on this subject. Zachary Macaulay had had in his hands the management of a vast West Indian estate which was worked by slave labour. He resigned that lucrative position because his conscience would not allow him to have anything to do with the system, which with his own eyes he had seen to be productive of so much crime and misery. William Wilberforce had identified his name and the name of his family with the abolition movement. Another family of great note, the Fowell Buxtons, had for a long time before and a long time after been the enemies of slavery in whatever form. Samuel Whitbread was devoted to the same cause —not a great many years have passed since his descendant, another Samuel Whitbread, aroused the House of Commons by his generous denunciation of certain practices which an English Government had thoughtlessly tolerated—practices which seemed to sanction the restoration of the fugitive slave to those who claimed to be his owners. Lord Grey and Lord John Russell were naturally to be found among the earliest opponents of slavery; and it had no opponent more earnest than Daniel O'Connell, the leader of the Irish people. The first great difficulty was to get up a strong, healthy public opinion on the subject. Any one can imagine, without too much racking of his brain, the kind of argument which would be applied by those who supported the system

It used to be said, for example, that England had no right to rob certain of her Colonies of an institution which was absolutely essential to the prosperity of the Colonies themselves. Without slave labour, it used to be declared, it would be impossible for the Colonies to be prosperous, because without it they could not hold their own against other places which permitted and encouraged the use of slave labour. Many even argued for the system in the interest of the slaves themselves. "Who," it was asked incessantly, "is to feed and clothe these poor creatures, if we remove them from the protection of their masters, who could only benefit by their labour under the existence of a slave system?" "How would it be possible," it was asked triumphantly, "for Europeans to toil in the sweltering, tropical rice-fields and cotton-fields?" Then again, it need hardly be said, that the accounts of cruelties practised on the negroes were indignantly denied. The masters were kindness itself to them, such was the voluble assertion; even if they had not been influenced by Christian feeling and sentimental humanity, a merely selfish care for their own interests would keep them from overtasking and punishing their poor slaves. All the talk about floggings and brandings; about the separation of parents from children; about women and girls treated like beasts of the field and scourged to their death; about runaway slaves being identified when captured because of the owner's brands upon their breasts; all these were idle tales, utter exaggerations such as only the fanatical fancy of an abolitionist could suggest.

In truth the English public had got into an easy jog-trot way of dealing in its mind and in its conscience with this question of domestic slavery. Numbers of the best and most respectable families of the country were known to have large possessions in the West Indies, and was it to be supposed that such men would tolerate for a moment a system which was fraught with such terrible consequences?

Then again a very taking argument was found by those who insisted that the workers on the West Indian plantations were for the most part better fed and cared for than the white slaves who drudged in an English factory or risked their lives in an English mine. This argument was especially telling because undoubtedly it had a certain amount of truth in it; and the Reformed Parliament had not yet seriously turned its attention to the condition of women and children in our factories and mines. As to the arguments drawn from the alleged humanity of the system, Zachary Macaulay and other experienced men supplied their friends with facts and dates and cases which no sophistry could refute to prove that the whole system was interwoven with cruelty and brutality of the most abominable kind. The public advertisements printed in Colonial papers concerning escaped slaves would have supplied proof enough of this, in the means of identification which were given—the backs marked with stripes, the breasts stamped with the burnt-in brand of the owner. How did it come about that English families of honoured name had great possessions in the Colonies where slavery prevailed and tolerated the existence of such evils? The answer was easy enough. Not many of the heads of those great families were at the pains of visiting their Colonial estates and thoroughly investigating the system for themselves. They found the slavery institution going on, and it did not occur to most of them that they were born to set it right. Most of them, even of those who actually went out and inspected their own estates, were willing to accept the reports of the managers and overseers whom they trusted, and did not take great trouble to discover what could very easily be concealed from their sight. Then, again, some of the owners of great estates did pay earnest attention to the condition of the slaves and did take care that so far as their own property went the negro worker should be fairly and kindly treated. But even to those men it was seldom borne in with any force of conviction that the system of slavery was a barbarous one in itself, and that merely to make the slave tolerably comfortable did not by any means dispose of even the principal objection to the odious system. It had not yet got clearly into the public mind that man's right to own his fellow man was, as Brougham said, "a wild and guilty fantasy." Therefore the pioneers in the Abolition movement had to set to work in the first instance to arouse the national conscience and to create a public opinion capable of supporting them in their noble and philanthropic efforts. But it was clear that with a non-reformed—that is to say, a non-representative—Parliament no strength of public opinion could have influence enough to carry the abolition of slavery. What did the unreformed Parliament care about the

WILLIAM WILBERFORCE, M.P.
(1759-1833.)

eloquence of Brougham, or Zachary Macaulay's array of facts and evidence, or the pleadings of Fowell Buxton and Wilberforce and Whitbread? The House of Commons of that day was not responsible to the English public. It was responsible only to the owners of the constituencies which held an overpowering majority in the House of Commons. At one time the Peers who sat in the House of Lords had, as owners of the soil in this place and that, a direct control over a large number of votes in what was ordinarily called the Representative Chamber. On such questions as that of Slavery and its abolition most of the landowners held firmly together. An interference with the rights of those who owned property in the West Indies might become but a precedent for an interference with the rights of those who held property in England; and the right of property seemed in the minds of many at that time to be something so sacred that no inquiry as to its operation, its origin, its justice, or its divinely appointed mission could be allowed without dread of the vengeance of Heaven. Then again there were difficulties of another kind. Some of the West Indian Colonies, and places also like Demerara, were governed directly from Westminster, and were in fact what are called Crown Colonies; but some, like Jamaica, for instance, and other West Indian islands, had a sort of representative system of their own and a kind of local parliament which managed their affairs. Now it was easy to imagine, and the imagination was only too well justified by the facts, that the Colonies which had any manner of local government would wax highly indignant at the thought of their representative system being interfered with by the meddling of philanthropists in the English House of Commons. Some of the strongest opponents of all representative systems in England were among the most eager to seize upon this form of argument and brandish it as their own in the faces of their philanthropic opponents. "Where is your consistency?" it was pertinaciously asked, sometimes in tones of mere anger, sometimes in tones of sarcasm. "You call yourselves Whigs and you are for ever clamouring about the independence of Parliament, and yet you want to take away from the parliamentary assembly of Jamaica or of Barbadoes the right to manage its own affairs." The Government made some efforts to compromise with some of the Colonies by issuing Ordinances which endeavoured to mitigate the severity of the slave system on the plantations. The Jamaica Assembly refused to accept the recommendations or orders of the Colonial Office and tried to mend the matter by passing an Act to mitigate the system; but the Act was of no practical use whatever, and the Colonial Office declined to sanction it. In Demerara there was something of a disturbance caused by the slaves in one part of the colony, who had heard vague news that their emancipation was coming, and on a particular day struck work, as we should put it in modern phraseology. This unhappy little movement was crushed by the planters with remorseless severity, and an incident occurred which was very timely, in the fact that it brought home to the mind of the British public a distinct idea of what the slave system could do in the way of hardening the minds of masters. An English Dissenting minister, the Rev. John Smith, was accused of inciting the slaves to insurrection. He was put in prison; he was made to stand a trial, which by its utter disregard of all the rules of evidence was itself an act of lawlessness; he was found guilty and sentenced to death. The court martial which tried him accompanied its judgment with a recommendation for mercy; but while some of the planters were humanely urging that the recommendation ought to be carried out, and others were insisting that the case of the poor minister afforded an opportunity for a stern example, to warn off other abolitionists, the missionary himself died from the effects of the imprisonment and the hard treatment he had received. The news of this death created a profound sensation in England. Brougham, Mackintosh, Lushington and other philanthropists stirred up the feeling of Englishmen to indignation. The Government were compelled by the force of public opinion to reverse the sentence of the court martial; and even when they had made this inevitable concession to the common feeling, Brougham went very near to carrying a resolution in the House of Commons denouncing the whole conduct of the trial.

A great meeting was held in London to agitate for the complete abolition of Slavery throughout all the British Colonies. Brougham brought on the whole question in the House of Commons and introduced a motion on the general subject of Slavery. Fowell Buxton did the same thing in the following session, and at last the Government began to feel that they must give way, and when Parliament met in 1833 there was a new man in the office of Secretary for the Colonies, Lord Stanley, the eloquent Lord Stanley as he may be described, who was afterwards the Earl of Derby. Lord Stanley was a man of generous emotions and of great parliamentary capacity. Macaulay said of him, that "with Stanley the mastery of parliamentary debate was an instinct." Short of the very highest gift of oratory, he brought everything to a great parliamentary debate which could claim success. He had a fine voice, a magnificent gift of language, and in especial that gift of phrase-making which has such a captivation for the House of Commons. Some of us can still remember him as Lord Derby in the House of Lords, and can remember that in that House he had, after Brougham's death, no superior; while in the two Houses of Parliament taken together he had no superior, and indeed no equal, except alone Gladstone and Bright. Lord Stanley was entrusted with the task of expounding to the House of Commons the policy of the Government with regard to the question of Slavery, and of proposing for the acceptance of the House certain resolutions in which that policy was to be embodied. He rose to his task with splendid effect, and no advocate could have better pleaded his cause; but the policy of the Government was not yet strong enough to satisfy the feeling of the country. Lord Stanley had five resolutions to propose—resolutions well worthy of being recorded, although in somewhat abbreviated form, if only to show that the high-water level of the Government policy was as yet but the low-

LORD STANLEY.
(*Lord Derby.*)

water level of the popular demand. The first resolution declared the opinion of the House, that "immediate and effectual measures be taken for the entire abolition of slavery throughout the Colonies, under such provisions for regulating the condition of the negroes as may combine their welfare with the interests of the proprietors." The second resolution proposed that "all children born after the passing of an Act of Parliament for this purpose, or who should be under the age of six years at that time, should be declared free, subject nevertheless to such temporary restrictions as may be deemed necessary for their support and maintenance." The third resolution started a new principle of compromise which found little favour in the eyes of the more advanced abolitionists. This resolution declared that "all persons then slaves should be entitled to be registered as apprenticed labourers, and to acquire thereby all the rights and privileges of free men, subject to the restriction of labouring, under conditions and for a time to be fixed by Parliament, for their present owners." The fourth resolution authorised the Government to advance, by way of loan, a sum not exceeding £15,000,000 sterling to provide against any loss which the owners of slaves might suffer by the abolition of the slave system. The fifth resolution merely gave authority to the Crown to establish a staff of stipendiary magistrates in the Colonies, and to provide for the religious and moral education of the negroes who were to enter into a sort of conditional freedom. The first and second resolutions passed easily enough, but the third became, as might be expected, a subject of much discussion. Mr. Buxton condemned the compromise contained in the resolution, and argued, with much ability, that the proposed interval of qualified servitude would do nothing whatever to render the negroes more fit to be entrusted with full and final freedom. Mr. Buxton received the powerful support of Lord Howick. Some of us can still remember Lord Howick when, as Earl Grey, he sat in the House of Lords, and was remarkable at once for his sterling abilities and for a certain independence of character which often made it difficult for him to submit to the restraint of official position. He was the son of the famous Lord Grey, Charles Earl Grey, the leader of the Reform movement in England, and by whom the Reform Bill of 1830 had been introduced into the House of Lords. Lord Howick, just before he spoke against Lord Stanley's third resolution, had given proof of his independence of character. He had been appointed Under-Secretary for the Colonies, and had resigned that position because he could not support or sanction the dilatory compromise recommended by Lord Stanley's third resolution. The Government had the powerful support of Mr. Thomas Babington Macaulay, afterwards famous as essayist and historian, son of the Zachary Macaulay who, as we have already seen, did more than almost any other man for the abolition of slavery. The younger Macaulay's arguments merely went to the effect that the transition from actual slavery to the condition of apprenticeship was at all events a decided step in advance, that it made absolute emancipation merely a question of a few

LORD MACAULAY
(1800–1859.)

defined years, and that it was probably about as far as the Government could, with safety to the very interests which they were striving to promote, venture to go just at that time. One interesting fact for all modern readers is that, in the course of the debates on the slavery question, Mr. Gladstone was heard for the first time in the House of Commons, which he had but lately entered. Mr. Gladstone declared himself in favour of emancipation, and had nothing to say in support of any slave system; but he was of opinion that slave emancipation must be accomplished gradually, that the slave must be educated and stimulated to spontaneous industry, and that the owners must be fairly compensated for the loss which the State was about to impose on them. Mr. Gladstone had not then risen to the high level of opinion on all questions concerning any manner of slavery to which he rose in his maturer years. Mr. Buxton proposed one or two amendments to the third resolution, but was prevailed upon, by the advice of some of his friends, to allow the resolution to pass so far as he was concerned, and without challenging a division. It is to the credit of Ireland that her popular leader, Daniel O'Connell, refused to listen to any terms of compromise. He had himself seconded Mr. Buxton's principal amendment, but he firmly declined to allow the third resolution to pass without challenge. He insisted on a division, and with so many opponents to contend against, the whole Tory party, the planter party, all the regular supporters of the Government, and many sincere friends of Abolition, who were, nevertheless, willing to listen to some sort of compromise; O'Connell carried forty votes with him out of a House of 324. This might seem a very small minority, and so it was numerically speaking; but those who understood the House of Commons saw then, as those who understand it will see now, that the principle which at such a time and in the face of almost unparalleled difficulty could secure forty independent votes was a principle to be reckoned with by prudent Ministers. The proposal of the Government for the £15,000,000 loan was fiercely opposed by all the friends of the planter interest. It was urged on behalf of the planters that the amount of the loan would not nearly cover the loss which Abolition would bring upon them, and there were not wanting many shrewd political go-betweens who hinted in public and explained in private that the loan was never likely to be repaid. The Government after a while began to think that there was little use in haggling over the settlement of so portentous a question, and they withdrew their proposal for a loan, offering instead an absolute gift of £20,000,000 sterling out of the national funds to recompense the planters for any loss to which they might have been put. The proposal was carried without a division. There was much difference of opinion about its justice then, and there is some difference of opinion even now. Why, it was asked, should the English populations be taxed to meet the losses which men might suffer who had to give up an odious trade, against which every Christian doctrine and every humane feeling alike protested? As well, it was urged, might the man who lived by the carrying off and selling of slaves claim compensation for his losses, when civilisation pronounced the decree that his infamous traffic must cease. Why should not the pirate plead for compensation when international law declared that he must no longer ravage the seas? Yet the Government on the whole was right in spending the money for the sake of obtaining a measure of abolition. England had grown up in a passive recognition of the right of men to have slaves in the Colonies and to make their profits out of slave labour. Two or three generations before the time of Wilberforce and Zachary Macaulay, it seemed quite a natural thing that the man who acquired West Indian property should be the owner of slaves, and nobody thought any the worse of him for it. England had allowed men to grow rich by slave labour all this time without, until quite lately, raising any strong moral protest against it. We have seen already how a public opinion had to be literally created in order to sustain any Government in an attempt to abolish the ownership of slaves and the making of fortunes out of slave labour. In the House of Commons, at the very time when the measure was introduced, there were many men, undoubtedly educated and humane, who did not see anything deserving of utter condemnation in the system of domestic slavery. More than a quarter of a century later still there were educated and humane Englishmen who got up on public platforms in London at the time of the great American Civil War to tell their audiences that the slaves on the plantations of Georgia and South Carolina were better fed and cared for than the workers in many an English factory and mine, as if that settled the whole question and left nothing else to be said.

On the whole, then, it was wise of the Government to get out of the entire controversy by throwing down £20,000,000 of the national funds to buy out the opposition of the planters and their friends. The Government had no difficulty in carrying their proposal through the House of Commons and the House of Lords. The House of Lords, it may be said, has rarely, if ever, put much difficulty in the way of any proposal which tends to benefit the owners of landed property at home or in the Colonies. A Bill was brought in by the Government which with some modifications simply carried into effect Lord Stanley's resolutions as adopted by the Representative Chamber. The principal modifications were the substitution of the larger gift for the smaller loan, and a reduction in the term of apprenticeship, from twelve years to seven in one category of apprentices, and from seven years to five in another. The Bill was then carried easily enough, and Slavery as a system was declared to be abolished for ever in the British Colonies. This, as has been said, was the first great work of the Reformed Parliament; and it will be readily acknowledged that a Reformed Parliament could not have started on its way with brighter omens than those which were shining from that first great success.

During the debates on the Slavery question the philanthropists, as they were contemptuously called —in other words, the opponents of the slave system —were constantly asked by the advocates of the planters, "Why don't you look at home? Why don't you turn to the condition of your labourers in your factories and your mines?" "If you will only think about their condition," it was urged, "you will have little time left to maunder and potter over the condition of the slaves in the plantations of Georgia and South Carolina. Don't you know that there is white slavery as well as black slavery, and that the white slavery is of your making, so far as these islands are concerned? Think more, then, of the white slaves of these islands, and less of the black slaves of Barbadoes and Jamaica." It would have been impossible that some Englishmen, and among them some of the leading opponents of West Indian slavery, should not have the condition of the white slaves of Great Britain brought to their minds long before the advocates of West Indian slavery had publicly taunted them with their indifference to the domestic evil. One of the principal opponents of slavery, in whatever form, was the late Earl of Shaftesbury—Lord Ashley, as he was at the time of the West India Bill. Lord Ashley had turned his attention from his early years to the condition of the workers in our factories and our mines. To him white slavery was just as odious as black, and he made himself, during his long career, a special champion of the white slaves. Many of us can well remember Lord Shaftesbury during his later days in the House of Lords. Some of us had the honour of his personal acquaintance, and all who knew him admired his thorough probity, his perseverance, and his practical philanthropy. He was not by any means intellectually a great man; and his was not, in politics, a commanding figure. He was a good speaker on any subject which he had thoroughly made his own and mastered, but he never shone as a debater in the House of Commons, where the years of his best activity were spent, nor even later on in the less eager and disturbing atmosphere of the House of Lords. He had, undoubtedly, some of the objectionable qualities of the fanatic about him. Where religious questions were concerned his opponents declared him to be a mere bigot, and it is certain that he had many strong prejudices, and was sometimes provokingly wrong-headed. All the same he was a genuine philanthropist, and when he kept to his own particular questions he was safe and steady as a rock. Lord Ashley made himself the pioneer of the parliamentary movement for the regulation of the work of women and children in factories and he succeeded after many efforts in obtaining the appointment of a Commission to inquire into the whole subject. The Commission took all the evidence available, and were able to present Parliament and the public with an array of indisputable facts to show the utterly destructive effect, both moral and physical, caused by the overtasking of women and children; and Lord Ashley at once set to work to agitate for the passing of some measures which would limit the hours and regulate the conditions under which women and children were to be kept to labour. His efforts raised a furious controversy, and brought up for settlement also an important economical question.

EARL OF SHAFTESBURY, K.G.
(1801–1885.)

The outcry raised by Lord Ashley's opponents was that his agitation was directed towards a legislative interference with the freedom of contract. There is a great tendency in the English mind to be governed by phrases, to turn some favourite phrase into an oracle, and allow it to deliver judgment in the teeth of whatever evidences and facts. For years and years after Lord Ashley had started his movement there were numbers of Englishmen filled with a fond belief that the words "freedom of contract" settled every question which could possibly come within the reach of the principle they were supposed to embody. Was it really proposed, Lord Ashley's opponents asked in stern accents, that Parliament should interfere with the freedom of contract; with the right of one man to hire labour, and the right of another man to let it out for hire? If a grown woman chooses to agree with an employer that she is to work so many hours a day at a specified rate of payment, what right has the Imperial Parliament to say that she shall not be free to sell her labour on such conditions as she finds suitable to her? If a man is willing to let out the labour of his children for so many hours a day at a specified rate of payment, has Parliament a right to step in and say that a man shall not deal with his own children as he thinks best for his interest and for theirs? Is it really proposed that the State shall assume the rights of paternity over all the children of the working classes in towns, and say when they may work and when they may not work? It did not seem to have occurred to many of Lord Ashley's opponents to ask themselves whether in such cases there is always any real and equal freedom of contract. The hard-worked artisan in a city with half a dozen children whom he finds it hard to support—is he really quite as free in the contract for their labour as the capitalist who offers to hire it, and who can get plenty of offers from others if some one particular working man declines to agree with his terms?

The opposition to Lord Ashley's measures did not always come, however, from hard-headed and hard-hearted economists who believed in freedom of contract because the freedom was all on their own side. Many men of the highest character and the most unselfish motives, many owners of factories who had through all their lives been filled with the kindliest feelings towards their work-people, were bitterly opposed to the whole principle underlying Lord Ashley's efforts. Such men were sincerely convinced, in many cases, that the economic laws settled, and alone could settle, every trade difficulty; and that Parliament could do no good, and could only do harm, by any attempt at interference with these inexorable influences. We have lost a good deal of our faith in the extreme beneficence of economic laws since that time, when so many were inclined to give to them a strength and a sanctity which mere instinct alone teaches us not to assign to the physical laws. We know that legislation cannot banish winter or prevent storms, but we know also that we can build houses to shelter us against the winter and the storm. At that time there was an opinion widely abroad among certain of the commercial and trading classes of England that a happy era was fast approaching when almost everything would be left to the settlement of the economic laws and the magic principle of freedom of contract. It was the dream then of many men, not otherwise much given to dreaming, that a time was fast approaching when the whole postal system of civilised countries would be left in the hands of private competition and freedom of contract. We have drifted far away from those ideas of late years, but they were just beginning to take form and strength at the time when Lord Ashley was making his beneficent efforts to regulate the labour of women and children in factories. Lord Ashley was supported by a great many landowners, for whom, naturally, the working of factories had no direct personal concern, and who could therefore afford to be philanthropic at the expense of the factory owners. These latter and their friends therefore turned fiercely on the landowners, and asked, "Why don't you call for the regulation of the working hours of women and children on your own farms and on your own fields?" They argued that the condition of wretched children employed in agricultural labour was far more pitiable, and far more deserving of the intervention of Parliament, than that of the well-paid and well-cared-for labourers in the factories, who were able to take care not only of themselves, but also of their wives and children. Then, again, the manufacturers urged that it would be utterly impossible to apply any general rule to all the various forms of employment in factories. Different kinds of productiveness required different hours and conditions of production. In some trades business came with an almost overwhelming rush at one period of the year, and was slack and short at another; how, it was asked, can you find any legislative rule which could apply with equal fairness to such labour and to the labour which went on steadily day after day throughout the year? In some trades the assistance of the women and children might be restricted without any serious delay of the labour of the adult men; in others, if the women and children were made to stop off the easy work which gave assistance to the whole production, the grown men would be compelled to let their work too come to a stand-still. How is it possible, it was asked, to get any Act of Parliament which can deal fairly with such diversified conditions of labour? and what can Parliament do if it tries its bungling hand at intervention, but make the condition of things infinitely worse than it was, until another Act of Parliament has to be passed to abolish by the common consent of everybody the misdirected and pernicious legislation which Lord Ashley and his philanthropic friends were striving to force upon the State? Lord Ashley and his philanthropic friends won the day nevertheless, and an Act was passed in 1833 limiting the work of children to eight hours a day, and that of young persons under eighteen to sixty-nine hours a week.

Lord Ashley persevered in the policy which, under his guidance, had proved so successful. At a later period he succeeded in obtaining the appointment of a Commission to inquire into the conditions and the results of the employment of women and girls in mines. The evidence taken before the Commission disclosed a state of things which shocked and startled even the most languid minds, and proved capable of bearing down all opposition in the end. The evidence brought out before the Commission revealed the fact that in several of the coal-mines, for instance, women were employed literally as beasts of burden. The seams of coal were often too narrow to allow any grown person to stand upright, and the women had to creep on their hands and knees, crawling backwards and forwards for fourteen or even sixteen hours a day. But they had not merely to crawl backwards and forwards, they had also to drag after them the trucks laden with coal. The trucks and the women were harnessed together after the simplest and rudest fashion—the usual plan was to make fast each truck to a chain which passed between the legs of the woman engaged in drawing it, and the chain was then attached to a belt which was strapped round her naked waist. The women who worked in these mines usually wore no clothing but an old pair of trousers made of the roughest sackcloth; they wore, in fact, the same sort of costume as the men, and the chief difference in their condition was that they were put to a lower and more degrading kind of work than that which was allotted to their male companions. These women were, indeed, literally unsexed; and not by any means merely in that metaphorical sense in which the word is sometimes now employed by the opponents of an agitation for woman's suffrage. It would be needless to attempt to describe the physical and moral evils which were necessarily produced by such a system.

Lord Ashley pressed on his movement, and it required some courage on the part of any Anti-reformer to stand up against it. Finally he succeeded in obtaining an Act of Parliament which prohibited for ever the employment of women or girls underground in the mines. The Act also declared that children under ten years of age were not to be employed in the mines at all; and the work of the children above ten years was limited and regulated. A number of Government officials were entrusted with the task of seeing that the provisions of the new Acts were properly carried into force. It may now be safely affirmed that the regulations for the employment of women and children in mines have worked with the most satisfactory results. Lord Ashley was not indeed the actual pioneer of the movement which he carried to such great success; many benevolent and enlightened men had worked before him for the same purpose and with the same high motives. But it is fairly to be said that Lord Ashley was the first man who forced the movement on the attention of Parliament, who directed the intelligence and the sympathies of the public in the right way, and who won the first lasting triumphs for the great cause of which he was so unselfish and persevering a champion. Since that time Parliament has been going farther and farther in the same direction. It has put forth its hand to regulate the hours and conditions of labour in workshops; it has interfered to secure for the workman some compensation for injuries caused by accidents amongst the machinery, where he was not himself by negligence or otherwise responsible for the harm he had suffered; it has asserted over and over again its right to interfere between employer and workman, where the workman is placed at an evident disadvantage by conditions over which he has personally no control; it will no doubt intervene, sooner or later, on behalf of the children who work in the fields, as it has interfered on behalf of the children who work in the factories; indeed, it may be taken for granted that Parliament will go on for a long time to come extending the application of the principle adopted in 1833 with regard to the hours and conditions of labour. It has been well observed that the course of legislation with regard to the labour of working men and working women has already passed through three distinct stages. The first stage was that during which no person not directly concerned troubled himself about the conditions of labour at all. The employer, it was commonly assumed, knew better than anybody else how to deal with those who worked for him, and even his own selfish interests, it was complacently argued, would have prevented any employer from overtaxing his workers too much; the man who harassed his work-people beyond their strength would never, it was contended, be able to get work enough out of them, and so, for their own sakes at least, the masters would deal tenderly with the man or the woman or the child. No doubt all this was true of many intelligent employers; and no doubt it was true also that a large proportion of the employers were men too humane and too kindly to exact over-work from those whom they employed. But with the competition that exists in all manufacturing communities, it is tolerably certain that the work standard of the exacting employers will become something like the common standard of the whole body. A sort of class public opinion; a sort of false conscience, is apt to be generated even among the kindliest of men who are rivals in the same work, where no check is imposed by the world outside. No check of any kind was employed in England before the agitation began which Lord Ashley conducted to success. Then there came a second stage, during which many an enlightened man endeavoured to set it up as a sort of scientific principle, that freedom of contract, and the higher forces of political economy, would manage everything for the best ; and that legislation would only make things infinitely worse by its unskilled efforts to interfere between capital and labour. Then there followed the third stage or period, during which it has come to be accepted that it is the right and the duty of every representative Parliament to intervene, wherever intervention is necessary, for the physical and moral protection of its citizens against evils which are not by any means a necessary part of the growth of civilisation. For years and years we, in these countries, have grown out of that condition of mental devolopment which can be satisfied with the dogma that freedom of contract and the laws of political economy may be trusted with the management of the world. Of late we have had legislation to intervene between the right of the landlord to make what terms he pleases with the tenant. Legislation lately has shown no respect whatever for the supposed rights of the owners of house property in the great cities to let out their houses under what conditions they please to enforce. We have had Act of Parliament after Act of Parliament to compel the owners of property to look after the sanitary condition of the houses and the rooms which they let out to hire. It ought to be said that both the great political parties of England have shown themselves equally ready to recognise the new principles; and the Tory Governments have been just as ready as the Liberal Governments to interfere between the employer and the workman, the landlord and the tenant, the house-owner and the lodger, where the welfare of the public called for such intervention. Indeed, the whole question may be said to have been long since lifted out of the sphere of partizan politics. Of late years there has been a sort of rivalry, and by no means an ungenerous or unwholesome rivalry, between Liberals and Conservatives, as to who should do the most for the protection of those who otherwise could do little to protect themselves. Naturally as the working population grew in numbers, in education, and intelligence, they have been able to assert their claims with an effect of which their forefathers could never have dreamed. Nor can it fairly be said that in later days the working population have made any unfair, or even unreasonable use, of their growing strength. Working men's associations and combinations have spread all over these islands, as they have in many other countries as well; and certainly we in these islands have no reason to say that the power of the working classes in their Trades Unions and their Leagues has often been misused. It is not so long since any combination of working men to come to a common understanding with regard to the hours they would work or the wages they would accept was an offence against the law, and was commonly treated as such, and followed by punishment of some kind, while, at the same time, the masters were perfectly free to agree among themselves as to the rate of wages they would pay, and the hours of labour they were to exact. At the time when Lord Ashley began his agitation the State did nothing whatever for the education of the working man and his children. Since that time we have had Acts of Parliament not merely establishing, but even enforcing systems of national education. The time is well within the memory of most of us, when it was a common saying that the principle of compulsory education was something altogether un-English, a sort of system which might suit Germans and such like, but could never be accepted among the freeborn population of Great Britain. The principle of compulsory education has done as much as anything could do to assist the working out of those enlightened laws which Lord Ashley did so much to call into existence.

Later on, a new and very peculiar interference between employer and employed was accomplished by Parliament. It did not strictly belong in date, or in actual conditions, to the factory legislation which

Lord Ashley and his friends accomplished; but in its character it forms a proper part of the same great movement for alleviating the condition of the hard-working and the badly-used. It would be somewhat too grotesque to speak of an interference between capital and labour, where the capitalists concerned were only the master-sweeps, and the labourers were the little climbing boys who were employed to cleanse the chimneys. Yet there was no reform accomplished by the whole philanthropic movement more cruelly needed than that which concerned itself about the climbing boys; nor were the sufferings endured on the West India plantations more revolting to every humane mind than those which were inflicted on the poor little helpless mites who were sent up the chimneys in all the towns of Great Britain and Ireland. Many readers now will require to be told what the system was, which, in this instance, called so pitifully for reform. To many of the younger generation the name of the "climbing boy" may convey possibly no manner of idea. Young men and women of this day never saw a climbing boy, never heard the cry of "sweep" come shrilly into the morning air from the top of a chimney. The trade of the climbing boy is believed to have been unknown to any country but the two islands under the English Crown. It seems to have begun in these countries somewhere about the opening of that eighteenth century to which we are accustomed to look back with an admiration which, intellectually, that century well deserves; but the intellect of the century did not apply itself over keenly to the study of the grievances of labour; and the romantic youths and maidens who watched the sun rise with poetic eyes, were not brought back to the practical rigours of life by the morning cry of the climbing boy. In most of our houses then the chimneys were high, narrow, and crooked, and at the opening of the eighteenth century statesmanship troubled itself very little about the sanitary conditions of house-building. It became after a while the settled conviction of all men and women who had what is called the practical mind, that there was only one way of properly cleansing a chimney, and that was by sending a little boy with a broom to climb his way through it and scrape down the masses of soot as he mounted up. The boy had to climb from the fireplace to the top of the chimney and to announce the accomplishment of his mission by crying out "sweep" when his soot-covered head and face emerged from the chimney-top. If the boy did not thus present himself to the open air and announce his triumph, who was to know that the lazy little fellow had not stopped his upward movement when half-way up the chimney and then begun to climb down again? The interiors of narrow chimneys are not provided with flights of steps for the convenience of climbing boys, and therefore the poor little creatures had to force their way up by working their elbows and knees against the different sides of the horrible structure. As a matter of course, their hands, arms, and knees were always abrased, and sometimes very severely injured, by this terrible friction with the internal masonry of the chimneys. Sometimes a chimney was so narrow that a poor little boy stuck fast in it, and could only be relieved from his awkward and dangerous position with much trouble. It often happened that when the boy was sent up the chimney was still hot from the recent use of the fire; and the poor little creature got severely burnt. It was proved beyond question or doubt that in many cases a boy who stuck fast in a still heated chimney, was found to be dead when at last he was dragged back to the hearth. The poor little creatures were dressed in a short gown of sacking, which was so covered with soot that it looked as if it never could be made clean again—and probably, indeed, no attempt was ever tried to make it clean again. The soot of one day's deposit was added to the soot of the former day, and after the first day or two the keenest unprofessional eye could not have detected any difference in the black accumulation. There was something peculiarly grim, pathetic and touching in Charles Lamb's description of the climbing boys as "these almost clergy imps." The faces of the poor boys were always covered and clotted with soot; and as the master sweep's countenance generally bore the same appearance, perhaps as a professional symbol, it was not likely that any great use was made of soap and water to give the climbing boy a short and futile interval of cleanliness.

For years and for generations people went on taking no notice of the sufferings of the little sweeps; the ordinary householder grew accustomed to them—it is very easy to grow accustomed to the routine sufferings of other human creatures—and it never occurred to most persons to ask themselves whether humanity could do nothing in the matter. The philanthropists, as usual, were the first to stir in the wretched business. These philanthropists would not even be content to let the master sweep do what he liked with his own climbing boys. In some cases they were literally his own climbing boys; for it was shown in evidence that master sweeps of the worst class had sometimes, for the sake of economy, employed their own children in sweeping the householder's chimneys. Here again the philanthropists were not to be daunted; they insisted on the right of legislation to interfere between the parent and his child when the parent set his child to the filthy and dangerous work of a climbing boy. The philanthropists carried their way in the end; they set about rousing public opinion, and they did at last thoroughly rouse public opinion. A mountain of evidence was produced to show the horrors of the system. It was proved that in many cases master sweeps had actually employed little girls to do the abominable work; and it was stated in Liverpool, and so far as we know never contradicted, that in one case at least a master sweep who had a wife, a young, small, and slender woman, passed her off as a boy and employed her in the climbing of chimneys. In many cases, as it was proved by uncontradicted evidence, when a poor child stuck fast in a chimney a master sweep declared that the boy was only shamming, that he was lazy and stubborn, and accordingly ordered a fire to be again lighted in the grate, so as to compel the unfortunate creature to mount the chimney in order to escape from the flames. Of course the extreme cases thus brought forward in the evidence did not even profess to be an illustration of the common ways of the trade. Many of the master sweeps were decent poor fellows enough: but there was the trade, under the same conditions as those which they had always known to belong to it; and when the respected and educated householder in the towns, when the county gentleman, and even the clergyman, made no objection to the practice, how was the poor sweep to find out that the employment of climbing boys was a disgrace to humanity? Such, however, it was; and so it was soon proved to be. The master sweep and his ways began to be a horror to the whole community. The Saracens, we read, used to frighten their naughty children into submission by threatening to hand them over to be dealt with by King Richard of England. In days that some of us can still remember many a rebellious infant was frightened into good order by the threat that he would be handed over to the master sweep. All sorts of stories began to get afloat about children of high birth and delicate nurture who were stolen away and sold to the master sweep; and, indeed, the master sweeps began to play in legend and in romance something like the part that had been played by the gipsies. A long time had to be spent in energetic agitation before anything practical was done by Parliament; but at last in 1840 an Act was passed which abolished the whole system. For a certain time, however, after the employment of climbing boys had thus been proclaimed illegal and with a penalty on it, the practice was still carried on clandestinely, and, indeed, in some places, with little or no appearance of secrecy. It put the ordinary householder out of his way to be told that when his chimney smoked he must refuse the friendly offices of the master sweep, unless the sweep came provided with a properly made mechanical brush for the purpose; and some of these average householders, being wedded to old-fashioned ways, thought the new system was only all nonsense got up by those interfering reformers. Public opinion, however, grew and grew, and at last became so strong and general and keen-eyed, that the most old-fashioned and reactionary householder could not let his neighbours suppose that he was a party to the torture of an unfortunate climbing boy. The machines adopted for the cleansing of chimneys proved to be able to do their work in a manner far more thorough and satisfactory than the most energetic poor child, who wore out his life under the old system, could possibly have done. Then we began to construct our houses on the more rational principles; and the sanitary laws came to be consulted, even in the construction of chimneys; and there was no longer any occasion for the sacrifice of the childhood of thousands and tens of thousands of little climbing boys. Society, therefore, it was found out at last, not only did not lose but actually gained by the intervention of the philanthropic reformers. As we have said, the old system is now forgotten by the present generation; but it is quite worth while to revive its memory for a while, if only to tell the story of those poor little martyrs to civilisation who were once regarded as so necessary a part of our domestic system that people never thought anything about their martyrdom, and did not even consider such a form of employment an evil serious enough to call for a moment's thought.

Another of the reforms, which like those we have already been describing, came in the wake of the great Reform Bill itself, was the abolition of the law of impressment for the navy. How long that law of impressment, or perhaps that custom of impressment which soon came to have the force of a law, had existed in our history, it seems hard, indeed, to decide. What we do know is, that in the days of the early Plantagenet Kings we find it alluded to as a system long in practice and accepted as one of the needs of our national defence. Of course it became, after a while, regulated by comparatively modern Acts of Parliament, which endeavoured to soften its rigours as much as it seemed possible to each succeeding generation of law-makers ; but the very laws which regulated it also of necessity acknowledged and sanctioned the custom of impressment for the navy. No regulation, no mitigation, could make it anything except a horrible grievance and a disgrace to a civilised system. The principle of all the Acts relating to impressment was that when the Government wanted sailors to man our ships of war, the authorities could seize men wherever they could get them, could capture them as if they were felons, and could send them for enforced service in the navy. It was not merely a plan of conscription like that which still exists in many civilised countries, applied to the recruiting for the navy. The system of conscription, whatever may be said for or against its merits, is a recognised system which applies to all citizens alike, which is one of the responsibilities of citizenship for which a citizen can prepare himself in advance, with reference to which he can mould his future arrangements, and for which, in most countries where it prevails, he is free to find a substitute. The impressment of men for the navy absolutely depended on the will or even the caprice of the authorities of that branch of the Sovereign's service. A sudden alarm of threatened war, a mere panic, a scare as we should call it in our days, might be enough at any time to set the naval authorities clamouring for fresh hands to the work, and enough to put the impressment system in active motion. It imposed not so much a civic responsibility as a penal responsibility, for the impressed men were simply captured and carried off as if they were escaped convicts who had to be haled back to prison. Naturally the seaport towns were the places where the naval authorities usually made their captures, and the stray seaman from a merchant vessel was preferred in all cases to the ordinary civilian. The impressment system was seldom carried on upon anything like a large scale without serious riot, and sometimes serious loss of life. The novel writer, the poet, and the painter, found ample and varied themes for their different orders of art in the workings of this extraordinary system of naval supply. Our romance is full of stories, some of which are read at the present day by young people who otherwise, probably, would never have known what the impressment system was. Many of these stories give pathetic accounts of young men pressed into the naval service just as they were returning from the church where they had been married, and sent off to serve at war on the seas, perhaps never to return to the scenes and the home of their birth. There is at least one touching poem which tells the story of a young man thus impressed on his wedding day, who serves on board all through the great wars with France in Napoleon's time, who returns a man of more than middle age, to find that his wife has long been dead, and that in his native town nobody even remembers his name. Poetic stories, somewhat like that of Tennyson's "Enoch Arden," gave an additional pang to the pathos, by describing the man as returning to his home to find his wife, who had long believed him dead, married to another husband; and picture him in despair returning again to the sea and the service, which had been his hardest enemies, but had now become his only friends. In many of Captain Marryat's novels, once the delight of all boys and of many grown men, we have vivid pictures of the riots caused by some sudden impressment in one of our seaport towns; of the press-gang, as it was called, forcing its way, cutlass in hand and pistols in belt, through resisting streets and lanes, which fire their shots from the windows as if they were striving to check the movements of a conquering invader; of houses defended literally from room to room; of desperate hand-to-hand fights; of women joining in the struggle; of wounds given and received; of death-blows given and received; and, finally, of the captured men dragged off as convicts might have been dragged to the galleys. At last public opinion began to be aroused to the horrors of the system. The philanthropic reformer, here, as everywhere else, was asserting his presence and making his voice heard. The Anti-reformers were stubborn. It was an article of faith with every Anti-reformer that it would be utterly impossible to man the navy if the power to impress men and drag them on board ship were not left unchecked and unchallenged in the hands of the authorities. To listen to such arguments might well have made a foreigner imagine that the Englishman of the poorer class, especially in the seaport towns, was a creature who detested the sea waves, who had not the courage to fight an enemy, and who thought it no concern of his even if the Frenchman were to invade the country. The Reformers, however, had their way in the end. They were now, in fact, riding on the crest of the Reform wave; and in 1835 the Government brought in a Bill to abolish the press-gang and to fix a period of five years as the limit of compulsory service in the navy. Since the abolition of the press-gang it has not been found that the naval service of England has been wholly neglected, or that English fleets are utterly without sailors to man them.

One genuine reform usually brings another in its wake. The abolition of the press-gang system gave the first fair chance for the abolition of flogging in the Navy. When the press-gang captured and carried off dozens of men from the lower quarters of some seaport town, it was not usual to require a certificate of character from the men who were thus compelled to do service in the fleet. It very often happened that the press-gang swept off among their captives many men who helped to form the mere scum of the streets in which they were found—men who had just come out of prison and were likely enough before long, if they remained on shore, to commit some new offence and be sent to prison once more. Men of this class, sent to do duty in the forecastle of one of our vessels of war, were not likely to exercise a moralising influence on the habits and characters of the sailors who were compelled to associate with them. The disorder, the bad example, the defiance of discipline which such impressed men brought with them, sometimes were infectious in their character, and helped to debase a ship's company. Crimes were undoubtedly sometimes committed which might excuse the maintenance of the flogging system in the minds of those who believed that anything but evil could possibly come out of such a system. The abolition of flogging in the Navy is an event which comes well within the recollection of most of us. Some of the most effective arguments made in the House of Commons against the use of the lash as a means of enforcing discipline was given by the owners of great merchant vessels or passenger vessels who happened to be Members of Parliament. These men pointed, again and again, to the example afforded by the discipline of the mercantile fleets. Take, they said, the great Atlantic lines of steamers, the great Pacific lines of steamers, the merchant steamers sailing every day from the port of London, from Liverpool, from Newcastle, from Glasgow, from Southampton, from every great seaport town—where can you find discipline better maintained? These vessels run all the risks that the war steamers have to face, except alone the rare risk of war, and it was not pretended even by the stoutest advocate of flogging that the blue-jacket was only inclined to fail in his duty when he had to encounter a floating enemy and a foreign flag. The finest of the merchant fleets had the additional disadvantage of having to carry on board great numbers of passengers, men, women, and children, whose presence at a time of threatened wreck must undoubtedly tend to increase confusion and to make the prompt and efficient discharge of the seaman's duty much more difficult. Yet the merchant vessels were able to do all their various and complicated work, although their captains were not entrusted with the right of flogging a refractory seaman. The arguments of the reformers prevailed in the end; and the flogging system was abolished both from Army and Navy. In truth it is hard to believe that any Government could have serious difficulty in manning either Army or Navy if reasonable and liberal measures were adopted to make it worth the while of a decent class of men to enter into either field of England's warlike service. The Navy, in especial, has always been dear to the general population of England. The Greeks of the classic days and the English of all days have been described as the only two peoples whose literature pictures the sea as a smiling and a tempting sight. The young Englishman of the poorest class has a natural fondness and aptitude for the sea; and although, even at the present time we have our occasional scares, and we find eager Anti-reformers crying out that the service is going to the dogs, there is no evidence to prove or even to suggest that England is likely to want seamen at any hour of national need. Time has proved that the naval service is all the better for the disenrolment of the press-gang and the abolition of the lash.

INDEX

A

Algiers, French conquest of, 199
Anglesey, Lord :—
  Catholic Emancipation supported by, 174
  Dismissal of from Lord Lieutenancy of Ireland, 181
Annual Register (1800), peace, International, prophecy concerning, in, 1
Army, flogging in, abolition of, 332
Ashley, Lord :—
  Mines, employment of women and children in, Act prohibiting obtained by, 316
  Slavery of factory workers and miners opposed by, 307
  Women and children, work of in factories, parliamentary movement for regulation of, pioneered by, 308, 311

B

Bonnymuir, battle of, 96
Brougham, Lord :—
  Appointment as Lord Chancellor, difficulties attending, 226
  Personal qualities of, 52

Brougham, Lord (*continued*) :—
  Slavery, abolition of, motion concerning introduced in House of Commons by, 295
  Slavery, system of, denounced by, 286
Burdett, Sir F., Catholic Emancipation supported by, 171
Buxton, Sir Fowell, slavery, abolition of, motion concerning proposed in House of Commons by, 295

C

Canning, George :—
  Anti-Jacobin started by, 114
  Career in Parliament, 114
  Caution characterising public utterances of, 135
  Death of, 146
  Early days of, 111
  Foreign policy of, 123, 129
  "Holy Alliance," policy respecting, 46
  Plymouth, speech at, 125
  Policy of, 122, 131
  Prime Minister, 144
  Tory attacks on, 141
  Secretary for Foreign Affairs, 117
  Under-Secretary for Foreign Affairs, 117
  Viceroy of India, 118

Caroline, Queen :—
  Conduct abroad, English opinion on, 74
  Lord Brougham as champion of, 74
  Public opinion concerning, 73

Catholic claims :—
  Cabinet dissensions on, 144
  George III. refusing to recognise, 28
  Sir Robert Peel opposing, 168

Catholic Emancipation :—
  Agitation for, 160
  Burdett's motion concerning in House of Commons, 171
  George IV. opposing, 161; pressed by Duke of Wellington to assent to, 183
  Lord Anglesey supporting, 174
  Sir Robert Peel supporting, 181, 189

Cato Street Conspiracy :—
  Edwards giving information of, 89
  King's reference to at dissolution of Parliament, 94
  Objects of, 89
  Political results of, 98
  Thistlewood :—
    Execution of, 97
    Part taken by, 90

Clare, Daniel O'Connell elected member for, 167, 190

"Climbing Boys" :—
  Employment of, Act forbidding, 325
  Hardships endured by, 321

Cobbett, William, teachings of, 50

Cochrane, Lord, 55

Congleton, Lord, *see* Sir Henry Parnell

Cumberland, Duke of, popular hatred for, 209

D

Dissenters, disqualification for seat in Parliament, 25; Act removing, 158

E

Eldon, Lord :—
  Peterloo Massacre, declaration concerning, 84
  Political creed of, 59
  Reform opposed by, 56

England :—
  Condition of at various periods during nineteenth century, 10, 18, 21, 47
  Revolution staved off by wars with France, 30
  War with France, public opinion concerning, 9

Europe, recasting of by Treaty of Vienna, 38

F

Fox, Charles James, political abilities and creed of, 14, 17, 25

France :—
  Algiers conquered by, 199
  Louis XVIII., accession to throne, 37
  Louis Philippe proclaimed King of the French, 202
  Press :—
    King and Ministers alarmed at criticisms of, 194
    Ordinances promulgated compelling silence of, 195
  Revolution :—
    Causes leading to, 193
    Names of great men associated with, 37
    Outbreak of, 201

G

George III :—
  "Benevolent despotism" of, political troubles resulting from, 27
  Death of, 35, 66
  Mental condition of, 32

George III. (*continued*):—
  Personal attributes of, 31
  Regent, son appointed as, consequent on mental condition of, 32
George IV.:—
  Accession of, 66
  Catholic Emancipation opposed by, 161, 184
  Character of, 66
  Death of, 202
  Extravagance of, 69
  Marriage to Princess Caroline of Brunswick, 73
  Retirement at Brighton, 75
Gladstone, Mr., abolition of Slavery supported by, 303
Glasgow, plot resulting in battle of Bonnymuir, 96
Greece:—
  Canning aiding in founding independence of, 136
  Turkish War with, England's part in, 141
Grey, Lord:—
  Cabinets formed by, 223, 276
  Career and character of, 284
  George IV. detesting, 182
  Resignation accepted by King, 273
  Slavery, system of, opposed by, 287

H.

Hanover, kingdom of, English hatred for, 210
"Holy Alliance":—
  Canning's policy regarding, 46
  Purposes of the Convention, 41
House of Commons:—
  King selecting places entitled to send representatives to Parliament, political consequences thereof, 102
  Ludgershall, member for, speech of, 104
House of Lords, abolition of proposals for, consequent on throwing out of Reform Bill, 261
Huskisson, Mr.:—
  Death of, 215
  Liverpool, speech of, 146
  Office resigned by, 149

I.

Ireland:—
  "Act of Union," passing of, 22, 26
  Rebellion of 1798, cause of, 22
  Wellesley, Marquis of, appointed Lord-Lieutenant of, 170

J.

Jews, disqualification of for seat in Parliament, 25

K.

Kotzebue:—
  Assassination of, 119
  Writings of, 119

L.

Liverpool, Lord, "Six Acts" introduced by, 60
Lyndhurst, Lord Chancellor, office resigned by, 186

M.

Macaulay, Zachary, slavery, suppression of, part taken by, 286
Mines, employment of women and children in, Act prohibiting obtained by Lord Ashley, 316
Monroe, President, doctrine proclaimed by, explanation of, 127

N.

Napoleon Bonaparte:—
  England receiving overtures from, 5
  England's struggle against, cost of, 18
  Imprisonment at St. Helena, 38

VOL. I.   23

Navy :—
  Compulsory service in, Act limiting period of, 330
  Flogging, abolition of, 332
  Impressment for, Act abolishing, 330

O.

Oath, new form of, Royal assent to, 158
O'Connell, Daniel :—
  Alliance with Democratic party in England and Scotland, 164
  Clare, election as member for, 167
  Re-election, 190
  Political career of, 162
  Slavery, system of, opposed by, 287, 303
Old Sarum, borough of, representation of in Parliament, 104

P.

Parliament :—
  Dissolution by William IV., noisy demonstration by mob, attack on Apsley House, 251
  King's message to, public opinion on, 209
    Debate on in House of Commons, 212
  New Parliament opened by King, 218, 253, 266
  Non-representative character of, 25, 102
Parliamentary reform :—
  Debate on, Duke of Wellington's speech, 219
  Government proposals concerning Lord John Russell's statement in House of Commons, 230
Parliamentary representation, anomalies of, 102
Parnell, Sir Henry, Select Committee to consider estimates for Civil List asked for by, 222

Peace, international, prophecy concerning in *Annual Register* (1800), 1
Peel, Sir Robert :—
  Catholic claims opposed by, 168
  Catholic Emancipation supported by, 181, 189
  Office resigned by, 186
  Tory obstructions to debate on Reform Bill systematically arranged by committee under, 257
Peterloo massacre :—
  Descriptive account of, 76
  Lord Eldon's declaration concerning, 84
  Political results of, 87
  Ringleaders, sentences passed on, 85
  Site of, Free Trade Hall erected on, 85
Pitt, William (the younger), political creed of followers, 13
Popular agitation, forcible repression of, Lord John Russell on futility of, 100
Press-gang, disenrolment of, 330

R.

Railway, Liverpool to Manchester, opening ceremony, occurrence at, 214
Reform :—
  Advocates of :—
    Brougham, Lord, 51
    Burdett, Sir Francis, 52
    Cobbett, William, 50
    Dundonald, Earl of, 55
    Fox, Charles James, 14, 17
    "Orator Hunt," 55
    Romilly, Sir Samuel, 52
    Sheridan, R. B., 17
    Whitbread, Samuel, 56
  Meetings in favour of, 64
  Opponents of :—
    Castlereagh, Lord, 63
    Eldon, Lord, 56
    Liverpool, Lord, 60

Reform Bill (first) :—
　Debate on first reading in House of Commons, 238
　Debate on second reading, 249
　Government defeat, 249
Reform Bill (second) :—
　Government majority on second reading, 254
　Government defeat, riots consequent on, 262
　House of Commons passing, 259
　House of Lords throwing out, public anger at, 261
　Meetings in favour of, 258
　Rioters executed, 269
　Tory obstructions, systematic arrangement for by committee under Sir Robert Peel, 257
Reform Bill (third) :—
　Amendment of Lord Lyndhurst carried by "Waverers," 273
　House of Commons passing, 269
　House of Lords passing, 277
　King pressed to create new Peers to secure passing of, 273
　Lord Grey's resignation accepted by King, 273
　Precedents created by passing of, 277
　Russell, Lord John, introducing, 269
　"Waverers" in House of Lords securing second reading, 272
　Wellington, Duke of, indiscreet speech made by on second reading, 272
Rick-burning, mania for, popular alarm at, 216
Roman Catholics disqualified for seat in Parliament, 25
Russell, Lord John :—
　Co-operating with Lord Durham in forming schemes for parliamentary reform, 228

Russell, Lord John (*continued*):—
　Parliamentary reform, statement of Government proposals concerning made to House of Commons by, 230
　Personal attributes of, 227
　Popular agitation, forcible repression, futility of, utterance on by, 100
　Reform Bill (third), introduced by, 269
　Reform Bill (third), phrase used by, during debates on Bill, various interpretations of, 281
　Slavery, system of, opposed by, 287
　Test and Corporation Acts, motion on in House of Commons, 152

S.

Shaftesbury, Earl of, *see* Lord Ashley
Sheridan, Richard Brinsley, oratorical gifts of, 17
Sidmouth, Lord, appointment as Home Secretary, 60
Slavery :—
　Abolition :—
　　Difficulties attending, 293
　　D. O'Connell supporting, 303
　　Loss to slave owners compensated by Government, 304
　　Lord Brougham introducing motion concerning, in House of Commons, 295
　　Mr. Gladstone supporting, 303
　　Motion in House of Commons concerning, by Sir Fowell Buxton, 295
　Arguments in favour of, 288
　Ashley, Lord, champion of white slaves (factory workers and miners), 307
　Bill abolishing, 306

Slavery (*continued*):—
  Brougham, Lord, denouncing system of, 286
  Grey, Lord, opposing system of, 287
  Macaulay, Zachary, part taken by in supporting system of, 287
  O'Connell, Daniel, opposing system of, 287
  Russell, Lord John, opposing system of, 287
  Smith, Rev. John, accused of inciting slaves to insurrection and sentenced to death, sentence reversed by Government, 295
  Stanley, Lord, five resolutions concerning abolition of Slavery proposed by in House of Commons, 299
  Whitbread, Samuel, opposing system of, 287
Smith, Rev. John, *see* Slavery
South American Colonies, formerly belonging to Spain, France projecting reconquest of, Canning's declaration concerning, 126
Spain, French invading, 125
Stanley, Lord:—
  Personal attributes of, 296
  Slavery, abolition of, five resolutions concerning, proposed in House of Commons by, 299

T.

Taxation, Canning and Huskisson remodelling system of, 142
Test and Corporation Acts, Lord John Russell's motion concerning in House of Commons, 152, 156
Thistlewood, *see* Cato Street Conspiracy
Treaty of Vienna, *see* Vienna

V.

Verona, Congress of:—
  Duke of Wellington attending as representative of England, 120
  Spanish affairs, Canning's instructions to Duke of Wellington, concerning, 121
Vienna, Treaty of:—
  England gaining little by, 39
  Europe how affected by, 36

W.

"Waverers," objects and methods of in House of Lords, influencing passing of Reform Bill, 270
Wellesley, Marquis of, appointment as Lord-Lieutenant of Ireland, 170
Wellington, Duke of:—
  Cabinet formed by, 146
  Character and qualifications of, 6
  Failure to form Cabinet, 275
  Fall of Ministry, circumstances of, 222
  Office resigned by, 186
Whig, meaning of term in time of Fox, 25
Whitbread, Samuel, Slavery, system of, opposed by, 287
William IV.:—
  Accession of, public feeling concerning, 203, 207
  Consent obtained for creation of new Peers on pressure of Lords Grey and Brougham, 276
  Familiarity of Lord Eldon's axiom on, 208
  Mob hooting, 275
Women factory hands, Lord Ashley promoting regulations affecting conditions of, 308

Y.

York, Duke of, death of, 145

www.ingramcontent.com/pod-product-compliance
Lightning Source LLC
Chambersburg PA
CBHW030807230426
43667CB00008B/1107